A CALLING

LUCY K. EVANS

LUCIDBOOKS

A Calling

Published by Lucid Books in Houston, TX
www.lucidbookspublishing.com

eISBN: 978-1-63296-511-0
ISBN: 978-1-63296-512-7

Special Sales: Most Lucid Books titles are available in special quantity discounts. Custom imprinting or excerpting can also be done to fit special needs. For standard bulk orders, go to www.lucidbooksbulk.com. For specialty press or large orders, contact Lucid Books at books@lucidbookspublishing.com.

This book is dedicated to my family.
Thanks for cheering me on. :)

Table of Contents

Acknowledgments

First, I would like to acknowledge my team at Lucid Books—Laurie Waller, Sarah Ray, Javan Hamilton, Megan Poling, and Alisa DeMarco. Thank you! This book would never have been possible if it weren't for you guys!

Next, I would like to thank my beta readers. To my siblings, Calla Evans and Seeley Evans, thank you both for agreeing to read the very first stages of my book. To Marcus Moore who read the fourth draft of the manuscript, thanks for pushing through the bad grammar and spelling. And thank you for forcing me to let you read it.

I would also like to thank all my friends. Thank you for encouraging me, being excited for me, and letting me know you had already preordered the book right after I was accepted. You guys are so amazing!

To Mom and Dad, thanks for believing in me and helping me on this journey. And thank you for giving me the space and time I needed to work on this book.

Calla, Seeley, and Rosie, thank you for cheering me on and getting excited for me. You guys are the best siblings ever.

And, of course, all glory goes to God, the creator of all things and the light in the darkness.

Prologue:
Fourteen Years Earlier

Gordon Hyde had just finished his special project, setting the colorful objects carefully into an ivory chest, when someone pounded on his back door. He glanced at the clock on the wall. Midnight exactly.

Miriam, he thought, shaking his head. *That woman would never be late.*

Gordon lumbered over to the door, swinging it open to reveal a figure in a dark cloak standing outside in the downpour. A strong gust of wind almost blew Gordon off his feet.

Stinkin' rain!

Gordon bowed respectfully toward his guest. "Good evening, Mistress Hunt."

The woman nodded her hooded head as Gordon stepped aside, inviting Miriam Hunt inside. Mistress Hunt strode into the "kitchen" that served as more of a workshop than anything. Tools for glass-blowing scattered the soot-coated counters; leather gloves hung on the walls.

"I can see you have been hard at work." Miriam's tone sounded disapproving as she nodded toward the mess.

Gordon blushed. "Yes, ma'am. I didn't get a chance to clean before you arrived."

A crackling blaze licked the logs in the fireplace that was built into the kitchen where an oven normally would be. It was easier having a fireplace there than running back and forth from the kitchen to the living room when Gordon needed tools. He had become tired of it after a while. After all, Gordon Hyde was no spring chicken anymore as he was nearing his early 80s.

"Where is it?" Miriam demanded, her voice low and eerie.

Gordon padded over to the ivory chest. "In here, m'lady."

"Hmm . . . open it."

Gordon unlocked the padlock with a difficult combination before he flipped open the lid, revealing a chest of colorful, glowing orbs. The spheres hummed softly. Mr. Hyde was proud to say that this was one of the best projects he had ever done.

Miriam slowly pushed back her hood, unmasking her face that was filled with awe. Gordon stared into her deep, brown eyes. They mirrored the multicolored glow of the chest. The woman reached for a magenta orb.

"Mistress Hunt," Mr. Hyde said.

"What?" she barked.

"Just . . . please be careful."

Miriam laughed before her voice became cold and stony. "Have they been tested?" she asked.

Gordon gulped. "Yes ma'am. They have."

Mistress Hunt nodded approvingly. "Then I don't see why I should be careful." She hungrily picked up the magenta orb. The woman cradled it in both palms, an evil smile spreading across her face.

She studied the spherical object before setting it back into the chest and closing the lid with a *thunk*. "I approve of your work, Gordon Hyde. For once, you have pleased me. Now I must get back home because I have a child to take care of—my sweet baby girl." Miriam sounded dreamy before pulling her hood up over her head. She picked up the ivory chest, walked to the door, and pushed it open. Rain sprayed into Gordon's home, but Miriam didn't seem to notice. She stalked to the middle of Mr. Hyde's backyard,

Gordon watched Miriam from the doorway. She reopened the chest and pulled out the magenta orb a second time. Through the fog, the sphere cast a purple halo of light around Miriam, illuminating parts of her face. She turned her head toward Mr. Hyde.

"Thank you," she said, inclining her head.

Gordon was shocked. Never in his life had he heard her say those two words. He nodded as she whispered into the orb. Purple lightning flashed, and Miriam was gone, leaving a circle of ash behind her.

Gordon sighed, wiping nervous sweat off his brow. Finally, Miriam was gone. Hopefully, she wouldn't notice she was missing an orb. Gordon had accidentally messed up this last one, and somehow it had doubled itself. So now there were two of them.

But he only had one of them. The second one had disappeared when Miriam knocked, and by disappear, he meant vanished into thin air. The bad thing was that he knew exactly where it went. And where it went was never supposed to even exist.

He walked into his dusty living room and rolled up the rug on the floor. He dabbed at his forehead with his shirt before he pried open the floorboards to reveal a wooden, rotted trapdoor. He grasped the rope attached to the decaying wood and pulled. A musty smell filled the room as he climbed down the rope ladder into the darkness below.

Gordon Hyde fumbled through the darkness to find his matchbox. He ran his hands over his worktable. Ah, there it was. He opened the small, rectangular box, pulled out a match, and struck it. He then lit an old oil lamp and set it on the table.

On the table sat a single object covered by a silk sheet. As he uncovered the orb, it flooded the room with light. The golden orb hummed with power.

This, though a mistake, was the best thing Gordon had ever created. But he feared that this orb would cause many problems in the future.

He scooped up the golden sphere and put it in a satchel that hung from a peg on the wall. He would have to hide the orb. Miriam would be after it. The golden sphere held power that none of the other orbs had.

Gordon scurried back up the ladder as quickly as his withered bones allowed. Before he made this journey, he needed to make a stop. It was his granddaughter's birthday. But since he would be stopping by so early in the morning, he would have to leave her gift on her doorstep.

* * *

Gordon quickly walked up the steps to his granddaughter's front porch. He peeked through the windows to see if the house was completely black before he pulled out a small box wrapped in gold paper. He set the gift down, propping it in such a way that she would be able to see who it was addressed to. He wrote her nickname on the tag instead of her real name. She would immediately know who it was from.

To my Brave Little Muffin. Keep it safe.

Gordon nodded his approval. That would most likely be the last time he saw his granddaughter's home. But now was not a time to be emotional. He had a job to do. If he didn't, Miriam would find the golden orb and have access to the real world. And that would put his Brave Muffin in danger. He couldn't do that.

Gordon miserably walked back to his car. He glanced back at the house one more time before he drove away. No one would see Gordon Hyde again.

CHAPTER ONE

A Thunderstorm
and a House

Alli woke early on a cool Saturday morning to find her boxer, Jax, barking at something that appeared to be lurking outside her bedroom window. She moaned sleepily and looked at the clock on her nightstand—4:15 in the morning.

"Jax!" Alli whispered. "Be quiet, please." The dog cocked his ear at the sound of her voice but ignored her otherwise. Alli sighed, throwing the blankets off her body before she stood and walked to the window. It was still raining outside like it had been for the past few days.

Alli watched as beautiful but rare purple lightning flashed in the distance. The night sky lit up, casting haunting shadows in Alli's bedroom.

All of a sudden, the house rumbled and shook for a split second. Jax began to whine, pawing at the screen in Alli's window before the tremor stopped as fast as it had come. It had shaken enough that her books and school assignments now lay in an unorganized mess on the carpeted floor.

Alli knew the tremor had not been thunder. Thunder couldn't have knocked books and homework onto her floor. No, it had been something much larger than that. There was a house being built a few roads away. Maybe part of the foundation had collapsed. But that wasn't likely. There was no way a collapsing house could cause such a tremor.

"Jax!" Alli cried desperately. "Please come over here!" She patted her bed urgently. The girl wasn't sure what had caused the house to shake, but it had definitely scared her, and she wanted Jax at her side.

The stubborn dog glared outside into the pouring rain, unwilling to listen to Alli's cries.

"It's okay, Jax. Nothing's out there," she reassured, attempting to convince herself as much as the boxer. She pulled her bright blue covers over her body and curled into a tight ball. "C'mon, pup." Alli yawned, beckoning him to her side.

Jax peered outside for another moment before reluctantly jumping onto the mattress and lying next to his mistress. Alli rolled her eyes, yawned again, and fell back into a dreamless sleep. She was too tired to think about what had shaken the house.

* * *

"Did you hear Jax barking last night?" Alli asked as she stumbled down the stairs the next morning. She squinted, willing her eyes to adjust to the light. The kitchen was flooded with the morning sun that shone through the windows. The sky had obviously decided to stop raining.

"No. Why?" her mom replied, setting a cup of black coffee on the kitchen table for Alli. Today, Mrs. Cormac had pulled back her golden hair with a yellow bandana. She wore her usual Saturday outfit—jeans and sweatshirt—instead of her weekly work attire, normally a skirt and blazer. In her hand she held a cup of black coffee, and Alli noticed her mom's nails were painted a cheerful yellow to match her bandana.

Mrs. Cormac grabbed a pan of roasted vegetables left over from the night before and scooped them into the trash can before dropping the pan into the sink.

"I don't know. He was freaking out about something, and I couldn't figure out why."

"Well," her mom said gently, "I'm sure it was an animal walking around our yard. We have to remember that Jax is very protective at times, especially during thunderstorms at night. You know how much rain scares him."

"Yeah," Alli said uncertainly. Mom hadn't mentioned anything about the small tremor, so maybe it was just a *very* realistic dream.

Mrs. Cormac chuckled and set a plate of eggs and toast on the table in front of her daughter.

"Thanks, Mom," said Alli, devouring her food and savoring the taste of the buttery toast.

When she finished, the girl wiped her mouth with her sleeve. "Can I ride around with Nicole today?" Alli stood and walked to the sink. She dropped her plate into the soapy water with a pile of other dishes.

"Have you asked her if she can go?" Mom scrubbed the plates and coffee mugs in the sink, using way more soap than necessary.

"No, but I can stop by her house on the way there," Alli said.

"Okay, fine, but make sure to look for cars." Mrs. Cormac turned around to look at her daughter, raising an eyebrow knowingly.

Alli rolled her eyes but smiled. "I know," and then she ran back upstairs to get dressed and grab her helmet.

* * *

Ten minutes later, after she got dressed and brushed her hair and teeth, Alli came back down to the kitchen to put on her knee-high rubber boots before racing to the shed at the back of their property to retrieve her dirt bike.

When the engine was finished warming up, Alli followed the dirt road to Nicole Andrews' house just around the corner.

"Hey, Alli!" shouted Nicole. She was sitting in a cushioned chair on the front porch, reading, when Alli pulled into Nicole's driveway. Nicole flipped a strand of long, dark brown hair over her shoulder.

"Hey!" Alli greeted her best friend after she turned off her bike. "Do you want to go to the track with me? I was on my way there and was wondering if you would join me." She took off her helmet and smoothed her blonde ponytail.

"Uh, sure," replied Nicole, tossing her hair again. "Let me just go let Mom and Dad know I'm going with you."

"I'll wait out here," Alli said as her friend walked through her gray, wooden door and into the house.

* * *

Alli heard the sound of her friend's KTM start before Nicole rounded the corner of her house and rode toward her. "Ready," shouted Nicole over the rumbling bike.

Alli nodded, slipped her helmet over her head, and started the engine again, her bike roaring back to life. She put it into gear, and they rode off toward the track.

* * *

"Want to race?" challenged Nicole excitedly, revving her bike for a more dramatic effect.

"Why do you even ask anymore, Nicole? I *always* want to race," replied Alli, revving her bike as well.

Nicole laughed and tore across the bumpy dirt track, leaving Alli coughing in the dust she left behind.

"Hey!" Alli shouted after her. "You never said 'go'!" She raced off after Nicole.

* * *

The girls rode all day until the sun settled down for the night and the moon shone. They sat on their bikes and watched the stars for a while.

"The stars are beautiful tonight," whispered Nicole as the stars reflected off her deep, brown eyes.

"Yeah, they really are," said Alli. Then she groaned, noticing the time on her watch. "I gotta go soon. I wasn't supposed to be out this late anyway."

"Lame," Nicole pouted. She suddenly changed the subject. "Did you feel something last night? It was like my bed vibrated for a minute. But I slept through most of it, so maybe I'm wrong."

"Yeah, I felt it too. I thought it could be the house that's being built near here. Maybe we could check it out." Alli cocked her head hopefully.

Nicole nodded. "I think we should. Besides, it'd be an excuse for you to get home late." She grinned.

* * *

Alli and Nicole were surprised to find that the whole frame of the house had been completely trashed and destroyed. No part of it had survived. "What happened here?" Nicole asked in a hushed tone, sidling closer to Alli.

"I don't know," Alli responded. "But what I do know is that whatever happened last night was not the construction workers up early. Look! There's light coming from over there." Alli pointed to the left of the driveway where the woods clashed with the side yard.

The two scrambled over rocks and rubble as they clumsily picked their way toward the dim light. Alli noticed there were burn marks mapping the rubble. Then it all clicked. The lightning from last night—it must have struck the house and made it catch fire. Alli scanned the pile. Sure enough, most of the wood was black and charred.

Nicole gasped and pointed at the top of a small tree. Alli looked and saw a magenta orb crammed between two branches. That was where Alli had seen the light. It had come from that glowing ball. And the glowing orb hummed softly.

CHAPTER TWO

The Magenta Orb

Nicole glanced at her friend, a look of fear and worry etched across her face. Alli wanted to be brave, so she started to plod toward the shimmery ball despite the small bit of fear bubbling in the pit of her stomach. She heard a strange sound, almost like whispering. It took Alli a moment to realize it was coming from the orb—like it was calling to her, urging her to come nearer, to reach out and touch it.

"Alli, no!" Nicole pleaded. "Please! We don't know what it is or what it could do to us."

Alli glanced back at her friend who, instead of looking horror-struck and worried, looked desperate. Alli didn't know what to do. She was very curious about the glowing orb, but she also cared about her friend, even if that meant she didn't get to do what she wanted. She valued friendship more than a sparkly, mysterious orb. Alli turned and left the glowing sphere where it sat in the tree.

The two scrambled back to their dirt bikes and rode home, parting when Nicole came to her road. "Bye!" Nicole said in a squeaky sort of voice before she hurriedly scurried inside.

Alli waved, but she was too late. The door had shut, and Nicole was gone.

When Alli turned onto her own road, she gasped. There were five cop cars and an ambulance at the end of the drive, all flashing their lights. Alli reminded herself not to worry too much because her 70-some-year-old next-door neighbors, Mr. and Mrs. Shirley, always seemed to have an ambulance on standby. But as she rode to the end of her street, Alli realized the ambulances and police cars weren't in front of the Shirleys' house. They were in front of hers.

CHAPTER THREE

The Kidnapping

Alli sped down the street as fast as she could to get back to her house. She skidded to a stop when she reached her driveway and dropped her bike onto the pavement, not caring a bit if the motorized vehicle suffered scrapes and scratches while she raced to the nearest crowd of police officers.

"What's going on?" she demanded of the closest cop who didn't seem to hear her. He continued to talk to the officers in a serious tone.

"What is going on?" she shouted again.

This time the man heard her and briefly glanced in her direction out the corner of his eye before he actually turned to speak.

"Uh, well, child." He stumbled over his words, kneeling down and resting his meaty hand on her shoulder. He cleared his throat. "We . . . received a call from your neighbors, you see. I think their names are Mr. and Mrs. Shirley. Anyway, they told us they heard a woman scream in your house. And a few minutes later, they saw someone, a figure in black, run out of your home and down the road." He pointed the way Alli had just come, in the direction of the dilapidated house. "He was carrying something over his shoulder—maybe a bag of some sort. Uh . . ." he paused and then sighed. "Your mother, we have been unable to find her. We have searched the house thoroughly. But sadly, there is still no sign of her—or the dog, for that matter. We saw him run off into the woods when we got here. He was barking and growling his head off." He ran his hand down his face, stopping to rub his short beard.

"No!" cried Alli. "She can't be gone! You're lying," she insisted stubbornly. Her mom couldn't really be gone. That was just some horrible prank.

Another cop, a woman this time, walked toward Alli and wrapped her in a tight embrace. "We don't know why she's gone, but we're planning on figuring that out," she assured Alli gently. Alli didn't care if a stranger was hugging her. All she cared about was finding her mom.

Alli leaned back, deciding that the cops were probably not lying to her. "Will you let me know if you have found anything?" she asked.

"Uh, yes," said the first officer. "About that—since your mom is, well, uh, somewhere, and your dad . . ."

"He and my mom are divorced," she said simply. "He lives in Michigan," mumbled Alli, embarrassed.

"Uh, okay." The man awkwardly shifted his weight from foot to foot. "Then where are you planning on going?"

"My friend lives right around the corner. I'll stay there for a couple of days until I figure out how to find my mom."

The man looked satisfied, nodding his oval-like face before turning to talk to the other officers in a hushed tone.

Alli took that as her cue to leave. She walked to the end of her driveway and lifted her dirt bike off the ground. She didn't bother putting on a helmet. She didn't care if she cracked her head on a rock if she slipped and fell. All she cared about in that moment was finding her mom and figuring out what in the world was going on.

* * *

"Alli? What are you doing here?" asked Mrs. Andrews, Nicole's mother, as she opened the front door of her house.

Tears pooled in Alli's eyes, but she wasn't able to turn her head away fast enough before Mrs. Andrews noticed. Her face was a mixture of pity and sadness as she swung the door open the rest of the way and gestured for Alli to follow her inside.

Mrs. Andrews sat Alli down in the living room. Their living room was one of Alli's favorite places. It was small but cozy and well kept.

Mrs. Andrews' mouth curved like she was going to say something, but at the last possible second, she offered something else. "Tell me what happened."

Alli told Mrs. Andrews everything, willing herself not to cry. Fortunately, she didn't. She just felt exhausted. When Alli finished sharing the devastating story, Mrs. Andrews' face appeared emotionless. She nodded and then stood, walking off to go fetch Nicole who was up in her room.

While Alli was waiting for Mrs. Andrews to return with her daughter, Mr. Andrews walked from the bathroom into the living room. "What's up, Alli?" he greeted her, grinning.

"Not much." Alli returned his smile, hoping he didn't notice how fake it was.

Nodding, he slipped on his leather boots, grabbed the car keys, and left the house.

Nicole and her mom walked back in a few minutes later, their expressions grim. Nicole sat beside Alli on the sofa, taking her hand in support while Mrs. Andrews settled down in the pinkish loveseat opposite the girls and crossed her thin legs.

"What did the cops tell you?" Mrs. Andrews eventually asked.

Alli stared into space as she answered Mrs. Andrews. "They told me that my neighbors heard a woman scream, and a minute later they spotted a figure in black running away through the backyard. The Shirleys informed the cops that the figure dashed in the direction of the house that was being built."

Maybe the orb and the kidnapper were part of the same scenario, Alli thought. She was itching to get back to the fallen house and her home to investigate. What if there was some clue the cops had missed?

Mrs. Andrews somehow managed to look thoughtful, worried, and afraid at the same time. "Well," she whispered, "I think all we can do is hope your mother stays safe and that the cops can figure out where in the world she is." She stood up very quickly. "But," she said, trying to sound cheery to lighten the mood, "we should get to bed."

So everyone retired for the night.

CHAPTER FOUR

A Surprise

Alli woke at midnight, completely drenched in sweat. She hastily kicked off her blankets in order to cool off, and then she lay on the floor of Nicole's pale pink room and patiently waited for her body to fall back asleep.

She waited.

And waited.

But that clearly wasn't going to happen anytime soon. And since she once more felt curious about the orb, she decided to leave the Andrews' home and venture back to the dilapidated house if she could accomplish it without waking anyone in the Andrews' household.

She crept down the stairs before she reached the dark living room where Mrs. Andrews, Nicole, and Alli had been talking a few hours earlier. She made her way to the front door and unlocked it. The lock gave a loud screech of protest before it clicked, and Alli opened the front door, a cold breeze whipping into the house.

"Uh, where are you going, and what are you doing?" Nicole slipped into sight just as Alli was about to close the door.

"I'm going to that house," Alli responded. So much for trying to sneak out of her friend's home without Nicole noticing.

"Not without me you aren't," insisted her friend, slipping out of her old, pink, cupcake slippers and into her shoes.

Alli sighed, defeated. "Fine. Come on, and get your dirt bike."

Five minutes later, the girls were pushing their bikes down the dirt road. They couldn't start them at Nicole's house or the powerful engines would wake her parents, and the girls would get caught. And there was no convincing cover story for why they would be out in the middle of the night pushing their bikes along the dirt road.

After they pushed their bikes away from Nicole's parents' house, they each swung a leg over their bike seats and started their bikes, stomping them into gear and riding down the dirt road until they turned left onto the cul-de-sac where the house resided.

When they arrived, Alli shut off her bike and ran toward the yard on the side of the house. A few animals scattered from under the rubble when she waded through the lumber and smashed concrete blocks. It hadn't taken long for the wild to claim this pile of rubble as their own.

Alli stopped when she came to the small tree. Her blood ran cold when she saw that the orb had disappeared. The only thing that seemed to indicate it had been there was a patch of black ash in the grass. The tree also looked strange. Alli brushed her hand across the bark, which flaked at her touch. "Nicole." Her voice quavered with fear. "The orb. It's gone."

CHAPTER FIVE

The Old Woman

Alli eventually persuaded Nicole to ride back to Alli's house to check if Jax had come back and see if there were clues the cops had missed. Nicole had been reluctant, but she agreed to go. They found nothing and ended up staying there the rest of the night because they didn't want to go back and get in trouble for leaving Nicole's house in the middle of the night. And besides, Alli still had a sliver of faith that her dog would come back.

Nicole, despite Alli's offer for her own room, chose to sleep on the old couch in the Cormacs' living room while Alli trudged up the stairs to her own soft bed. She felt mentally and physically drained. She wasn't all that surprised, considering she had discovered a weird glowing orb, her mom had been kidnapped, and later had found that same orb had mysteriously disappeared without a trace.

Something was going on. Alli just wasn't sure *what*.

She fell asleep quickly, regardless of Nicole's booming snore from a level below.

* * *

A loud *crash* woke Alli again for the second time in two nights. She leapt out of bed and ran down the steps, skipping three at a time. When she made it to the living room, she found her mom's favorite crystal lamp shattered on the floor and Nicole standing in a corner, eyes wide and knees knocking together with fear. Nicole shook her head toward Alli, trying to send a message.

Alli, not noticing what her friend was trying to say, walked into the room, oblivious that there was a shadow in the shape of a human standing in the corner.

"Alli!" Nicole squeaked, pointing to the other side of the room.

Alli turned her head to see what Nicole was pointing at.

There was, indeed, a shadow, and it was quickly advancing on Alli's best friend. It then formed into an old, hunchbacked, leathery-skinned woman who pulled out the glowing magenta orb the girls had seen in the tree.

Before either girl could react, the old woman said something that sent chills down both Alli's and Nicole's spines. To Alli's ears, it sounded like babbling. But Alli somehow knew it wasn't. She heard and saw Nicole pleading with the woman to stop, and then she screamed. Alli witnessed her friend's form become a blur before it was absorbed into the orb, the echo of her begging scream still ringing in Alli's ears.

The woman chuckled to herself like she did this every day, and then she whispered to the orb again and turned her attention toward Alli.

Alli, shaken out of her state of shock, moved faster than she would have thought possible. She bolted back upstairs and locked herself in her room, shoving her dresser against the door for protection. The old woman pounded on the thin wood from the other side, trying to break in.

Alli grabbed her backpack and shoved in it items she thought would be helpful in her escape. In the pack were a headlamp, an atlas, a few sets of clothes, and money.

She froze, realizing the house had become eerily silent. The old woman wasn't banging on her door anymore.

Maybe she left, Alli thought, glancing around her room.

Glass shattered, and her skin felt like knives had pierced her skin. She cringed in pain, glancing at her arm and seeing it had a shard of glass deeply embedded in it. She scanned her room and found a rock the size of a baseball on the ground in the middle of her carpeted floor.

Alli heard the old lady's cackle again and then saw her float through her window and into her room as if there was an invisible rope holding her up. But there wasn't. The woman landed on the floor without a sound and pulled the orb out of her pocket.

Without thinking, Alli ran forward and slammed into the thin and surprisingly frail, old woman, making her fall backward into the wall. The girl heaved her dresser out of the way with astonishing strength and ran down the stairs, through the kitchen, and out the front door.

CHAPTER SIX

On the Run

Alli felt like she had been riding for centuries. She didn't exactly know where she was going; she just knew she was going *away*—somewhere safe.

One thing she hadn't thought to pack was something to light a fire, a warm blanket, and food, which was really stupid of her. She would be camping on the cold, hard ground that night with no fire and nothing to eat.

It would be bloodcurdling for two reasons. One, there was a possibility the old woman would find her again, and two, she had never gone camping by herself. She had always gone with her parents so they could shelter her from the unwelcoming darkness of the gloomy nights. But that was before they had separated. Alli hadn't been camping since.

An idea occurred to her. If she was lucky, she would pass a gas station and maybe buy food and something to light a warm fire.

Unfortunately, gas stations don't normally sell blankets, so she would have to figure out something else.

"All right, I'd better get going so I'll get at least five hours of riding before it gets dark," Alli reminded herself.

She started her bike and drove down the long stretch of dirt and gravel until she turned onto a smooth, paved road. She continued to go south-ish, and when she didn't find a road that went the direction she needed, she rode through the lush, damp forests, creeks, springs, valleys, and rocky trails.

At one point, Alli tore through a crop farm, speeding as fast as her bike would let her, but she wasn't going fast enough. A lanky farmer with a goatee shook his pitchfork at her, yelling some not-so-very-nice words that she would've gotten in *big* trouble for using.

In Alli's haste to get out of the farm before the angry man caught her, she accidentally drove through a small area of crops and a vegetable patch, earning more angry yells from the farmer.

She laughed as she sped off into the woods on the other side of the small estate where she could still hear the angry farmer yelling rude curses her way.

CHAPTER SEVEN

The Cold Night

That evening, Alli stopped by a small brook and concluded it would be a good spot to stay that night. She could hear the owls hooting, the coyotes yipping, and the bullfrogs gruffly croaking, each animal playing their part in the music that would later lull Alli to sleep.

She washed her sweaty, dusty face off in the spring, feeling deeply refreshed before she dug a hole in the soft mud next to the brook. Water started to steadily stream into the hole through the mud, filtering the cool water. Alli used her hand to scoop up the brown liquid, savoring the coolness it sent down her throat. It tasted earthy, but it was better than drinking water straight from the brook that held bacteria.

She had trouble falling to sleep later that night because of a strong fear that bubbled and churned inside her, knowing there was a chance the dark figure would find her again. She wouldn't be surprised if that was exactly what had happened to her mom.

Alli curled up on her pitiful, small pile of leaves she had made. Her arm still throbbed from the glass that had sliced her skin. She was positive there were still shards embedded in her arm. She had pulled the largest shard out of her flesh only to realize that there were more shards.

She shifted her position on the leaves, gazing through the small parting in the thick trees to look up at the stars. Alli loved to wonder what could be out there. There were many new galaxies and planets that had never been discovered. She spotted the Little Dipper, and then she found the Big Dipper. After that she found her favorite star of all—Alpha Centauri.

Alli watched the stars until she fell asleep.

* * *

When Alli woke the next morning—not sure exactly what time it was—she could see a tiny sliver of the sun peeking over the horizon. She heard the birds chirping and the locusts still quietly buzzing. She spotted a doe and her two sweet fawns lapping up water from the stream. The two fawns were gangly-legged and sprinkled with white spots. Alli smiled and thought they were some of the cutest animals she had ever seen.

"Well, besides Jax when he was a puppy," she whispered to herself, her smile fading when she realized she missed the dog—her stocky, overprotective, paranoid boxer. She hoped she would be able to see him again one day. She wished her dog was here with her, but she was on her own.

She glanced back at the doe and the two gangly fawns and smiled once again as she stood and brushed the dirt off her hands. She really needed to find a gas station for food.

Alli walked over to her bike and started it, twisting the throttle to get the engine used to the chilly wind. She put her bike in gear and drove east, hoping to find a nice paved or even gravel road to ride on instead of steering through the woods. For a bit she had to push her bike, maneuvering around fat logs, round trees, spiky bushes, sharp rocks, and thick undergrowth.

Alli rode, pushed, and maneuvered for what seemed like decades before she reached a lonely, gravel road. The girl felt like she could collapse where she stood and cry with relief. She was tired, sticky with sweat, and shaking with hunger. Now that there was a gravel road, she could ride smoothly and hopefully find a paved road that would lead to a gas station.

Alli decided she should probably check how much gas she had left since she had been working her bike so long and hard. Her shoulders slumped when she found there was only about an eighth of a tank left. If she didn't find a station soon, her bike would die, and she would have to walk the rest of her journey.

Disappointed, discouraged, and chilled, Alli sped down the road again, her stomach growling louder than the roar of her bike.

CHAPTER EIGHT

The Second Meeting

S ometime later, Alli's bike began to slow and soon after stuttered to a halt. A sob welled up inside of her, but she choked it back, reminding herself that she had to be strong.

That was hard. Really, really hard.

Alli couldn't push her bike the whole way. She would have to leave it where it had died and walk. *It'll be fine*, she tried to convince herself.

Alli started her trek.

* * *

Hours passed before she reached a gas station. The place was in the middle of a small town in the middle of nowhere. Alli was so excited to finally be able to put something in her stomach that she ran inside and started grabbing any type of food in her reach until she realized she needed to pace herself and save money for other important things. She walked around looking for a pack of lighters. Instead, she spotted a box of matches and was about to pay for her items when she realized that surprisingly, there were blankets in one aisle. After a pause, she snatched one before she walked back toward the cash register where a suspicious old man was eyeing the matches in her hand.

Alli happily stepped outside the building 10 minutes later, carrying one bag full of food and another with a blanket and a box of matches. She didn't know where she should go. She was debating on trekking back into the woods and setting up a temporary shelter. Her second option was to keep walking, stopping only to eat and rest.

Alli had reached the edge of town and was walking on the side of the dirt road when all of a sudden she thought she saw movement out the corner of her eye. She turned her head slowly, hoping it really wasn't what she thought she saw.

But when she looked in the direction where she had seen movement, there was nothing there. Alli shrugged and continued to pad through the rocks. But there it was again, a dark shadow that seemed to flicker in and out of sight. She turned again and again, but there was nothing out there but the edge of the road and the trees that lined it. Alli turned in a slow circle, studying the landscape around her just to be safe.

Leaves rustled, and she turned just in time to see the old woman pulling out her magenta orb again, babbling into it. A cruel smile spread across her face as she approached Alli, who realized with a jolt that the plants and trees turned black and withered when the cloaked figure passed and crept closer and closer to her. Before long, the lush greenery withered and turned black like it had been baking in the hot sun. Only the trunks of trees survived.

The girl ran as fast as her legs could carry her. She saw another shadow form into another old woman who carried a pale yellow orb. Again, any vegetation in a radius of 10 feet of the second figure died. Alli yelped. There were now two people after her instead of one. And anything green withered before it turned to ash

Alli jumped over a log and ran into the dense woods. She looked back only to see that the old ladies were trailing behind her, both swiftly floating. The log Alli had just leapt over became black. She stumbled and almost hit a tree but quickly regained her footing, sprinting as fast as her burning, aching legs would carry her.

The old women were rapidly gaining on her. The figure carrying the magenta orb whispered into it while she glided across the blackening landscape.

Alli's heart raced with fear. She had never before felt it beat so fast.

She ran on and on for what seemed like hours but was really only minutes. She could spot the second lady with the pale orb but not the first woman. Alli kept a sharp eye, knowing that the lady was smart and wouldn't let Alli go without a fight.

She heard the sound of a plane engine flying overhead and stole a quick glance at the sky. It was a Cessna, the same model she had been studying.

Excitement zapped through her body. The plane had flown low, but she could tell it was now ascending into the sky. That only meant there was a small airport nearby. That idea gave her enough energy to run toward the direction the plane had come from.

Sure enough, there was a small airport filled with Cessna 172 planes. She sprinted toward the newest and cleanest looking plane. She didn't have time to do the exterior check, and she didn't want to risk having any problems while she was trying to escape.

Alli yanked open the door to the cockpit and climbed in to start the plane. It ran for a few seconds before the engine sputtered and shut down.

"No, no, no, no." Alli tried to start it again, and fortunately, the engine kept running.

Alli began to taxi down the runway before she gained speed and took off, leaving the two old ladies and the withering forest behind her.

CHAPTER NINE

Flying the Cessna 172

A lli sighed with relief. She finally was able to rest her legs, even if it meant she was attempting to fly a plane.

She switched the craft to autopilot, not even sure where she was going. Alli just knew she was going away from the old hags, and then she would figure out how to find and rescue her mom and friend wherever they were.

After amusing herself by digging through the plane's storage compartments, Alli had a large pile of items that could more than likely help her survive on her journey. They included a backpack, an empty canteen, more matches, and a parachute.

She stuffed the matches and canteen into her own backpack and set it next to the parachute. Alli had no plans to use it, but she decided it was better to be safe than sorry.

The girl wandered back to the cockpit and checked the radar, which was still thankfully clear. She also glanced at the gas gauge,

It was down to half full, which, in Alli's opinion, was a good thing. She didn't really want to add falling out of the sky to her to-do list. She observed that the sun was going to rise in the next hour, which meant she needed to find a place to land. She hoped she would land the Cessna fairly well and not end up crashing it into a tree.

The girl scanned the landscape around her, watching for a flat place to land. There was a small lake below her with a flat, rocky bank. She doubted the plane's landing gear would survive the rough landing on the rocks, but she had to try. She switched the plane off of autopilot and angled the nose of the craft down, beckoning it into a steep dive.

The ground flew up to meet her in a matter of seconds, and at the last minute, Alli pulled the plane out of its descent and leveled out with the ground. She screamed when she noticed the craft was speeding toward a large rock and that she was about to crash the Cessna. Alli braked the plane, and the landing gear hit the bank roughly, sending the craft airborne for a second or two before gravity pulled it back down again, the boulder halting its travel.

Alli groaned and unbuckled herself. Her neck was killing her, and she felt her back pop when she stretched and stood on the uneven floor of the cockpit. She picked up the backpack of supplies, but she left the parachute since the plane would not be meeting the sky any time soon.

Stumbling out of the cockpit, she walked toward the boulder she had crashed into. She sighed, knowing she would be in big trouble if anyone knew she had stolen and destroyed the Cessna. The nose of the craft was caved in, fitting the exact shape of the aggravating rock. It looked like she was stuck on the ground from now on.

Alli walked to the edge of the crystal clear water and looked at her reflection. She rubbed a hand down her grimy, dirt-crusted face and decided it was time to clean herself.

She walked around the plane to the edge of the lake and waded, clothes and all, into the freezing water. Her teeth chattered, but she walked deeper. Soon, Alli was swimming, her fingers numb and her lips blue. She inhaled deeply before she plunged under, rubbing the dirt and grime out of her hair before surfacing again. It felt so good to bathe after going for about a week without cleaning herself. Alli submerged herself multiple times, splashing water everywhere and laughing because this, though the water was seriously cold, was the most fun she had had since she left home.

When Alli felt like she was about to freeze to death, she paddled back to the rocky shore where she lay on a patch of warm grass that grew in the sun.

Her stomach growled, and Alli reached for her bag of food and grabbed two water bottles. She closed her eyes in delight when the cool water slid down her throat. She sighed and was about to lie back down when she heard a stick snap behind her. Alli started to turn around, but before she had the chance, someone grabbed her from behind. A second figure walked up to her and pulled out yet another orb, but this one was neither yellow nor magenta. This one was navy blue, and the figure whispered to it.

A searing pain coursed through Alli's body, and she screamed, trying to scramble away from whoever was holding her. The last thing she remembered was halfheartedly stomping on her captor's feet. Then she lost consciousness.

CHAPTER TEN

The Order

lli could hear voices. She couldn't make out whose voices they were or what they were saying, but she knew they were voices. Some of them were high-pitched, and others were deeper and rattled Alli's eardrums.

They seemed to be getting closer.

Closer.

Closer.

Closer.

She could hear her heartbeat getting louder in her ears.

Louder.

Louder.

Louder.

Alli's eyelids fluttered.

She blinked a few times, her eyes slowly adjusting to the light. The girl scanned her surroundings, noticing that she seemed to be in an old, half-dilapidated factory. The windows were shattered. There were broken, old machines littered everywhere, scattered on the floor and hanging from chains from the ceiling.

She attempted to move her arms, but her body was bound to a freezing aluminum chair. Alli struggled with the cord knotted firmly around her wrist, twisting her hands back and forth to slip free from its taut, painful hold.

"You will never be able to escape," said a gruff, gravelly voice that echoed throughout the dark building. "You are just as foolish as your mother," a hooded figure whispered in her ear, the warm breath sending tingles down Alli's spine.

Alli wanted to cry out, but she clamped her mouth shut. She refused to give the hooded figure the satisfaction of surprising her.

The figure strode away from Alli and quietly crept to the other side of the room before turning to face the girl again.

"Where's my mother?" Alli asked, her eyes shooting sharpened daggers at the hooded character.

"Oh," the figure sneered. "Well, I can assure you that *I* didn't take her. A different individual was assigned to do that. You can meet that person if you like. LeRouge!" the figure shouted, not even waiting for an answer.

Another black-cloaked figure walked through a wide door into the main part of the factory and stood next to the first figure.

"Show them who you are," spat the first.

Alli's captor nodded and reached for her hood, pulling it down and showing her face.

Alli gasped.

The woman in front of her had scars that created a map on her face. Some looked fresh because parts of skin still had a pinkish hue instead of the pearly, shimmery white color of old scars. Her hair was flaming red, her eyes were gray, and her expression was dark. Alli decided that this lady was someone you should not play around with.

"Alli, this is Dementia LeRouge," the first figure introduced the young woman, laughing evilly as if this were all a joke. And Alli wished it was. But she knew it was not, even though everything that was happening was weird.

"I think it's about time you met me," the first figure decided, pulling down her hood as she spoke. Alli thought she might pass out from the dizziness that overcame her.

It was Nicole's mom, Mrs. Andrews.

Alli's mouth opened and closed a few times with a loss of words, and realization swept over her. Mrs. Andrews had lied to Alli. But what struck Alli harder was that she had also lied to her daughter and her husband.

"Why?" Alli said, tears pooled in her eyes. She had always thought of Mrs. Andrews as a second mom.

Mrs. Andrews pulled her hood back over her lying head. "Because I wanted to protect my daughter," she stated simply, shrugging her shoulders.

Alli burst out laughing, partly because of a deep sadness and partly from the shock and anger that swirled inside her. Mrs. Andrews cocked her head to the side. "What's so funny?" she asked, her voice failing to mask her surprise at Alli's sudden outburst.

"Nothing," Alli said, trying to breathe and calm herself to enable her to act like she was taking the situation seriously. "It's just that you absorbed your daughter into a glowing orb that makes you feel like you're burning from the inside out. And now you think that was the best way to protect her?"

"It was, and she knew it," Mrs. Andrews said lazily, setting a pale hand on her hip. "You see, Nicole has been in the Order ever since she was born. She was born to change the world. That was my plan all along for her." Mrs. Andrews gave Alli a cold, sly grin that shone with greed and hate. "Her name was never Nicole," she continued, "just like my name was never Sienna Andrews."

Alli opened her mouth to interrupt, but the apparently-not-Mrs.-Andrews rushed forward and put her pale, clammy hand over Alli's lips. "Let me finish," she hissed.

Alli nodded, her body shaking from fright and shock.

"Good." The not-Mrs.-Andrews folded her hands neatly and stepped back from Alli. "My real name is Miriam Hunt, and my daughter's actual name is Essence. You will be pleased to know that she helped plan your mother's kidnapping. Isn't that great? We put the magenta orb up in that tree, burned down the house, and let Nicole go with you to the track so you would be distracted. We needed you to stay out late so we could put the plan into full swing. Our original plan was to have you touch the orb and then be sent here, but Essence, being ever so loyal, told you not to." Miriam smiled cruelly.

Tears streamed down Alli's cheeks as her heart ripped in half. Essence had known. She had helped plan the kidnapping. She knew that all of this would happen. And the worst part was that she had been distracting Alli, not going out to have a fun Saturday together. Alli had thought they were friends. "Before we lock you away," Miriam continued, "I need to introduce you to the rest of the Order."

At once, people in dark cloaks seemed to melt out of the shadows, forming in an even line behind Miriam Hunt. Miriam addressed the figures in the same babbling language that Alli had heard from the ladies who had hunted Alli and Nicole, but this time it was mixed with a series of clicks and snarls. Each figure lowered her frayed hood, all revealing their identities. The women wore cold, stony expressions. Some had scars on their faces like LeRouge, but none were quite as violent.

"Alli, I would like you to meet Drace Vexx, Law Maganti, Leeta Everbleed, and Voss Scarlet. We also have Raura Umbra and Ilene Tempest, who you both know to be the one who took Essence or, in your case, *Nicole*." She spat out the name with pure disgust. The two creepy, old women looked like the oldest of the whole Order. The other women were quite a bit younger. "And now we have Lyra Bloodworth who works with our six trainees—Mortica Rex, Brie Redwood, Sisuca Barkridge, Demonia Demholm, Zephyr Marth, and Samantha Crypt."

Alli noticed that all the women except the trainees had orbs of their own that were all different colors. It either meant they did different things or the colors matched their personalities. Alli saw that LeRouge's orb was pure black, so Alli hoped the colors didn't match their personalities.

"Now, Alli, you will be a good girl and be cooperative. Give us your pendant," Miriam Hunt said, holding out her fragile-looking hand while tapping her left foot impatiently.

Pendant? Alli thought. *I don't have a pendant, let alone wear one.* Alli never wore jewelry of any type. The only things she wore were earrings, but she didn't count that as jewelry.

Miriam's features hardened when Alli didn't answer. "Go on, girl, hand it over."

"I don't have it," Alli said meekly.

Miriam's face went red. "Yes you do. Give it to me!" she demanded.

"No!" Alli refused.

Miriam's expression became full of anger and hate. *What a foolish girl. She should know better than not to listen to Miriam Hunt.*

Miriam strode forward and grabbed Alli's wrist. "Stupid girl! If you don't give it to me now, you will stay locked up until you do or decide to help me find it. Ilene, do it!" she shrieked.

The old woman who took Nicole, or Essence, walked forward and mumbled into the magenta orb. Pain coursed through Alli's veins before she again sank into the thick blackness.

CHAPTER ELEVEN

The Dark Room

A lli woke again. Wherever she was, it was pitch black. It also had a damp smell to it. She patiently waited for her eyes to adjust to the heavy gloom before she sat up and stretched. Her arm was still sore from where the shard of glass had penetrated her skin, but thankfully, everything had scabbed up and stopped constantly oozing.

It took a moment for her memories to come flooding back to her. She remembered how Essence had betrayed her. How she had known about the kidnapping. How she had lied . . . lied . . . lied. Now this was Alli's question: is her so-called friend trustworthy? After everything that had happened, Alli would say no.

Alli stood and kicked the stone wall. Her big toe throbbed on impact, but she felt a bit better. She started walking slowly around the edge of the dark cell. She noticed that the floor started to slant as she curiously crept forward . . . and fell into a deep, dirty pool of water.

Alli could feel slimy trash and junk floating around her body, and she shivered. She couldn't feel the bottom of the freezing pool as she frantically tried to grab the edge of the stone floor she had fallen off of.

Alli hoisted herself out of the water and flopped onto the floor where she wrung the water out of her shirt before curling up against the brick wall. This had to be worse than a regular old jail cell. Miriam Hunt had overdone herself. Alli lay there feeling useless until she was unable to stay curled against the wall any longer. She got up and continued to trail a hand across the rough brick walls, minding the deep, disgusting pool until she felt the coolness of a smooth iron door. This was a room from which no one was supposed to be able to escape. She was trapped, and the lurking feeling of claustrophobia swirled in the pit of her stomach.

The room seemed eerily quiet except for a slight breeze that blew into the room with little puffs. It was almost nerve-racking. Alli had never felt a silence as dense as this. She was used to an ongoing noise, which usually aggravated her, but now she didn't think the racket she was used to hearing was so bad. In fact, she craved it. She needed it. But there was none to fill the small room.

Alli tripped on something on the floor. She stumbled and fell, catching herself on her hands and knees. "Ow!" she yelped. She wondered how many times she was going to get hurt. She had already broken her record for the most injuries in a week.

Alli turned so she could sit on her bottom and inspect what she had tripped on. It was moving, which surprised her. It wasn't moving a lot, just rising and falling in short little puffs. "Like the wind," Alli whispered. There wasn't wind coming in at all like she had assumed; it was just this thing on the floor making that noise, which led Alli to the conclusion that it must be a person.

She reached out to touch the figure on the floor. It kept breathing as Alli slowly felt around in the dark trying to flip it over on its back so she could see the face.

She peered at the face of the person, noticing it was again another woman. She looked oddly familiar, but she wasn't Essence. She was too long and a tad bit wider as well.

The woman stirred in her sleep, and Alli saw her eyes flutter. "Um, hello?" Alli whispered, hoping the woman heard her.

The woman rolled toward Alli, her eyes glinting in the dark light. "Who . . . are you?" The woman coughed, and Alli winced, knowing from experience that was a really bad cough to catch. The woman was obviously sick and in need of medical assistance, though Alli had none to give.

"My name is Alli," she told her, sweeping the light-colored, sweat-soaked hair out of the woman's dim eyes.

The woman bolted upright, coughing before she stuttered, "Alli?" The woman reached for Alli's face, tenderly landing her warm fingers on her cheeks. Actually, her fingers were *too* warm. "My daughter?" the woman asked.

Realization jolted Alli like the plane crash. No wonder the woman's demeanor felt so familiar. "Mom?" Tears welled in Alli's eyes before they silently streamed down her pale face. She leapt into her mother's arms and held her tightly, making sure she wasn't squeezing too hard. She didn't want to make her mom's condition worse than it already was.

They sat together for what seemed like forever, but Alli was good with that. She had really missed her mom. But now Alli knew everything was going to be okay.

Finally, Mrs. Cormac pulled away and looked Alli in the eyes, love and hope dancing and leaping through her soft expression. She ran her hands from Alli's shoulders down to her hands, stopping to tenderly hold them. Alli winced when her mom did this, but she quickly tried to hide it. Her wound from the glass was still in the healing process.

"What's wrong?" her mom asked, concerned.

"Nothing. My arm hurts a bit, but it's nothing to be worried about," Alli assured, covering her sore arm with her opposite hand. She knew she was trying to reassure herself just as much as she was trying to convince her mom.

"Let me see." Mrs. Cormac gently pulled Alli's hand away, revealing the torn-up arm. She put a hand over her mouth in shock. "What happened, Alli?"

"The woman with the orb came to our house and took Nicole—whose name is actually Essence, by the way—and she's part of the Order. I tried to hide in my room, but Ilene Tempest, the old woman, threw a rock at my window and shattered it to get in. That's why my arm is like it is. But it's nothing to really worry about," Alli finished.

Her mom raised her eyebrows. "Is that all you did?" she asked suspiciously.

"Well, I kinda stole a plane and crashed it into a boulder when I was trying to land on the bank of a small lake. But that's a minor part of the story that you need to forget." Alli's face broke into a grin despite the large blast of guilt that tore through her heart. Her mom had always taught her not to steal, and Alli had done just that. What she had done was wrong, and she knew it.

A soft moan filled the room, and Alli jumped. Mrs. Cormac laughed at her daughter's reaction to the ghostly sound. "That's just Nicole," her mom reassured.

"You mean Essence?" Alli corrected. She tried to keep the venom out of her voice.

"I'll get it one day," her mom said softly, nudging Alli's shoulder. "She's been here two or three nights. It's hard to tell the exact time in the ongoing darkness. I don't know exactly why she's in here, but she's your friend, so maybe she'll tell you."

"She's not my friend," Alli said as she walked over to where she heard the noise that had come from the center of the room near the edge of the nasty pool of water.

After a minute of blindly searching in the darkness, Alli found Essence sitting on the floor, leaning her back against the wall. "You knew about the kidnapping?" Alli questioned. She didn't have time for greetings.

Essence's face paled. "Yes," she answered, twisting her hands.

"And you helped plan it?" Alli glared at the girl. "You distracted me for a whole day so the others could carry on with the plan? Your mom said the Order burned down the house and put the orb in that tree, hoping I would reach out and touch it and be sent here." Alli's voice slowly became a harsh yell.

Essence shamefully stared at the cold, hard floor. "I'm sorry," was all she said. Alli noticed that she didn't deny any of the facts.

"Yeah, sure." Alli hated Essence at the moment. In anger, Alli kicked the stone wall again as hard as she could. "Ow!" she muttered under her breath. But again, it felt good to kick something.

Alli looked into her friend's face, checking to see if Essence felt badly about anything she had done. Tears streamed down Essence's pale cheeks, but Alli didn't care. She left her friend where she sat and walked back to sit with her mom.

Alli dropped to the floor angrily. "Miriam said something about a pendant?"

Mrs. Cormac sighed. "Yes. Alli, I need to tell you about that," her mom said, pulling a thin chain over her head with a small black pendant swinging wildly from it. "This is the Path," she explained.

"Wha . . ."

Mrs. Cormac held up her hand. "No," she said gently. "Let me finish. This pendant was given to me by my grandpa years ago. Actually, I got it just before you were born. I had no idea what it was for. The only thing the note said was "Keep it safe." I don't fully understand its properties and what it's supposed to be used for, but Miriam Hunt will search to the ends of the earth for it, so now it's time to give it to you." She put the pendant over Alli's head, the charm resting just below Alli's collarbone.

"But why me?" Alli asked curiously, cocking her head. All anger toward Essence had faded as she had forgotten about her.

"Because I am incapable of protecting it any longer and I am positive it will be safer with you. Besides, you told Miriam Hunt you didn't have it, so that would give us a greater advantage because now you do."

CHAPTER TWELVE

The Dream

A lli hadn't realized how exhausted she was until she was put in the room. She now lay down on the cold floor and propped her head on her arm. She patiently waited for sleep to slip over her, but it never came.

Alli lay there for what felt like hours, waiting for sleep to take her into the blissful rest she loved. Essence had curled into a tight ball at one end of the room and was already asleep. Alli's mom stayed in her own corner, saying she didn't want to get Alli and Essence sick. Finally, after shifting her position about a billion times, Alli drifted off.

* * *

Alli dreamt she was back at home, laughing with her mom and playing her favorite family game. Her mom was winning, of course, as she always did in that game. Jax was there, too, licking their faces and putting his massive paws on their shoulders. They were having a good time.

The scene shifted once more, and Alli was flying on a carpet. She laughed as she studied the landscape below her. There was the vast, blue ocean and a beach with hundreds of people playing in the sand. And then she was falling. She screamed as she fell.

Down.

Down.

Down.

She was about to splatter on the sand, but instead, she fell through the face of the earth like a glitch in a video game.

Alli was now walking through a dark cavern, and the smell of mold polluted the air. She glanced around the tunnel frantically, taking in her surroundings. She saw that Essence was at her side. "Look," dream Essence said as she pointed at the rough ground of the dark cavern. There was a glowing, circular trapdoor that had opened beneath them. It led into a dark cavern below.

The girls jumped through the opening to the cavity below. The pendant around Alli's neck pulsed softly. The farther they walked through the cavern the more harshly it vibrated until it started to burn her skin.

Alli tried to take the necklace off, but it wouldn't move; it just kept burning her skin. Essence helped by trying to unclasp the chain, but it wouldn't budge. It was like it had fused together. Tears streamed down Alli's cheeks, but there was a light that shone at the end of the dark tunnel. Alli was sure they were almost to the end of the terrifying cave. The girls eagerly ran toward the light, longing to escape the growing gloom. Alli's vision blurred, and the pendant's burn intensified.

But as the girls came closer to the light, the world started to flip again, and Alli slammed against the tunnel wall. "No," she whispered, sinking through the rough stone that liquefied like water.

She was back home again in the kitchen, sitting at the bar while her mom made sugar cookies for Christmas. Alli was organizing the sprinkles by color, and her mom was telling her about all their holiday plans.

Mrs. Cormac had just closed the oven door to bake another batch of cookies before setting the oven mitts on the marble countertop. Alli's mom was in the middle of a sentence when her eyes rolled back into her head and she sank to the floor, her chest no longer rising and falling.

* * *

Alli gasped and sat up, sweat dripping off her brow. It took her a while to remember that she was still in the dark room, not at home. Essence was still sleeping, snoring softly.

Alli wandered to the other side of the room where her mom was lying. Thankfully, Mrs. Cormac was still breathing, and a wave of relief washed over the girl. It had just been a dream. There was nothing for Alli to be worried about.

The girl moseyed around the still dark room, looking for a way she could get Essence and her mom out of the room. She searched and searched, scanning the walls for anything that could get them out. So far? Nothing.

"*Alli?*" called a soft, sweet voice.

Alli shook her head, sure she was imagining a voice calling her. She glanced back at her mom and Nicole. They were both still. She shrugged, continuing her search.

"*Alli?*" whispered a scratchy voice.

Alli whirled around, positive she had actually heard a voice.

Her mother stirred. Alli stared at her for a moment. Mrs. Cormac's lids fluttered before her gray eyes scanned the room and rested on Alli, a weak smile forming on her dry, cracked lips.

Alli's eyes welled up, a few fat tears pouring down her cheeks.

"Mom?" she asked.

"I'm here."

Alli ran over to her mother, kneeling down and wrapping her in a fierce hug.

"Mom," Alli pulled back from Mrs. Cormac. "I'm going to get us out of here, okay? One way or another."

Her mom opened her mouth to speak, but she was abruptly cut off by a resounding bang and squeal that filled the musty room. It sounded like metal scraping across metal. The iron door creaked open, and Miriam Hunt stepped inside.

CHAPTER THIRTEEN

Night

"Up," Miriam Hunt commanded, dragging her half-asleep daughter off the floor. "Alli, get your mother."

Miriam briskly escorted the group of three out of the room into the main factory area where Alli had been before. They exited the old building and went outside. The first thing Alli noticed was that the trees and undergrowth were all dead. But it wasn't just where cloaked figures were. It was everywhere. Every last bit of plant life had been turned to ash. Only the sturdy tree trunks were standing, charred and ashy. The second thing Alli saw was a long row of flatbed trucks and black SUVs waiting for their arrival.

Miriam strode toward the first black SUV where intimidating men in dark, swaying cloaks were stationed, impatiently waiting. Miriam had earlier explained to them that they would be transporting "packages," so they were quite surprised when Miriam Hunt sauntered toward them leading her pale daughter and two others. They had assumed they would be transporting a few supplies in crates and boxes, but not *people.*

"Alli, meet Night, a group that works alongside the Order." Miriam introduced them, and men in black cloaks lined up beside the trucks. "And this is Everit Graves, the leader of Night." The man called Everit Graves grunted. He was a short man, shorter than Alli, but what he didn't have in height he made up for in width. Alli couldn't tell much else since he was enfolded in a black hood.

"So where are you taking us?" Essence asked, feebly peering around her mom's shoulder. Essence was only a little bit shorter than Miriam Hunt.

"You are not going anywhere, Essence. You will stay with me," Miriam stated. "Unfortunately, this facility was sighted by a family camping in the woods last night. We failed to catch them, so the Order is temporarily moving to the evacuation center, which is safely hidden and guarded next to the Night facility."

"Great." Essence's shoulders slumped, and she looked at Alli, a blend of fear and annoyance pushing through her normally guarded expression. Alli scowled, still reluctant to forgive the girl.

Miriam Hunt rolled her eyes at Essence. "LeRouge and Miss Vexx will be your escorts. I'm having them keep a sharp eye on you. As for Alli and her mom, they will be riding in the prisoner SUV for transport," she smiled cruelly. Alli shivered at the unwelcoming thought of traveling in the dark vehicle with no way to escape. Alli was desperately forming a rough plan, and if all went well, she could escape and find help.

Graves grabbed Mrs. Cormac by the arm and led her, limping, over to the black SUV. Surprisingly, he carefully helped her into the daunting vehicle. Alli was proud of her mom since she still gave Graves a cold glare when he started to shut the back door of the car. It took all of Alli's willpower to not laugh when Everit didn't notice. She hid her smile behind her hand.

The girl watched LeRouge and Vexx lead Essence into a second SUV. Alli realized she was the last person in their group who hadn't been put into one of Night's transports.

She had to make sure no one was eyeing her so she could put her plan into action. Alli scanned the crowd of black-cloaked figures. From what she could tell, no one was looking her way. She heard her name spoken at one point, and someone hooked their thumb her way, but they didn't look at her.

Alli bolted, swiftly running for the dead forest at the other end of the factory building. She pumped her legs as hard as she could. By now people noticed she was escaping, and they yelled, scrambling to catch her.

Adrenaline must have kept Alli going because her legs and body were not tiring. She would go back and rescue her mom and Essence; she just couldn't do it yet. But she would. She promised herself.

By this time, members of Night had seen her and were making a desperate effort to chase after her. A few hopped in empty pickups and made a break to cut her off before she made it to the dense woods. They were too late. Alli was already in the forest, dodging black logs and small, charred trees that slowed her down.

Dogs howled, and Alli glanced behind her. A pack of gray, snarling wolfhounds chased after her. The only things slowing them down were the chains the men from Night held. The dogs were hunting her.

Alli kept running.

The blackened woods she had plunged into were not very deep because she could already see a winding country road at the other end of the patch of forest. But she had another idea, one that was more dangerous than what she had just done. The Order and Night would pass this road in search of her because they knew this was the way she had run.

Thankfully, she had lost the dogs for now, so Alli crouched stealthily behind a tree when she reached the edge of the road and waited.

CHAPTER FOURTEEN

Alli's Plan

Alli listened to the roaring engine of a black truck speeding down the road.

For her plan to work, she would have to be patient and stealthy. Fortunately for Alli, the clouds overhead were rapidly turning from a depressing gray to black as night. She predicted that the seemingly heavy downpour would start in the next five minutes, which would be perfect for her for two reasons. First, the rain would blur the windshields on the trucks, making it harder for them to see the landscape before them. Second, the rain would make so much noise that hopefully the drivers wouldn't hear her.

Sure enough, the rain started to fall in large drops that splattered noisily on the ground and on Alli. It didn't take long for her clothing to get soaked through. She despised the feeling of wet jeans. She scowled.

A truck came into her view, and she focused all thought on what she was about to do in the next minute. Her body shook with excitement and fright. She estimated about 50 ways this plan could go wrong, and she did not want to see what happened if she *did* mess up.

As the truck sped past, Alli jumped out from behind the tree as fast as lightning and leapt onto the rear of the truck. Her chilled hands scrambled to find a handhold on the slippery truck bed.

When Alli thought she was going to slip from the truck and tumble into the mud, she caught hold of the lip on the tailgate. She heaved herself up and over, tumbling into the bed with a loud *thump*.

What she didn't notice is that all the other trucks from Night were flatbeds, and the vehicle she had hopped into was a pickup.

Alli shook her head, trying to clear the dizziness that overcame her. "Hope they didn't hear that," she muttered to herself.

Alli silently but quickly crawled to the back window of the cab and peeked inside. The driver and one other man, strangely dressed as ordinary people, sat alert in the cab. Alli figured the people from the Order and Night were dressed in disguise. That made sense, but how they had changed clothes so fast Alli didn't know. She looked away from the window and sat down on the truck bed. Now she just had to wait until they drove back to the evacuation center. Alli stared up at the sky, the gray stretching on forever and ever. Her eyelids became heavy, and despite the pounding, freezing rain, Alli curled into a ball and fell asleep.

CHAPTER FIFTEEN

Kind Strangers and a Voice

"*Alli,*" someone softly called her name like a whisper carried by the wind.

"*Alli,*" they called again, their voice sweet and melodious.

"*I'm waiting for you.*"

"*Come to me.*"

"*I'm waiting for you . . .*"

Alli's eyes opened in a flash, her chest rising and falling rapidly. She blinked a few times, allowing her eyes time to adjust to the dim light. Someone had been calling her. But who? She quickly scanned her surroundings, but there was no one there. She was sure someone was calling her.

She started to panic when she noticed she was in someone's living room. She should have been in the black truck instead of lying on a worn, brown, leather couch surrounded by old antiques perched on shelves. The last thing she remembered was falling asleep in the rain. So where was she now?

She wearily sat up on the couch, the sound of the sweet voice still echoing in her head. The girl didn't hear anyone or see anyone, and she wondered if she was alone.

Alli jumped when a door slammed and an elderly woman walked in, her hair pulled back with a bright red bandana that kept her graying hair away from her face. The woman spotted Alli and gave her a wide smile. "Hello." She walked across the room toward Alli. "How did you sleep?" she asked.

"Good," Alli mumbled, trying to keep alert. But this was hard since the woman's welcoming smile melted all of Alli's suspicions.

"Well, we left some food in the kitchen for you. We were going to wake you up, but we decided to let you sleep." The lady smiled again. "Sorry I didn't introduce myself when I came in. My name is Jean Hayes. And my husband's name is Charles."

"Oh, um, I'm Alli Cormac," she told the lady, blood rising to her face.

"What a nice name!" Jean complimented her. "Would you like me to bring you your late lunch, or would you prefer to eat in the kitchen?"

"I'll eat it in the kitchen, thanks." Alli stood up and yawned again. She realized she hadn't actually slept well since flying the plane before she was kidnapped by the Order. She was thankful that Jean and Charles had let her come and stay with them until she had a plan to rescue her friend and mom.

Alli missed them. She missed how her mom was always strong and encouraging during the hardest times. She wished she were at home in her own bed, curled into a ball and reading a book. But right now, Alli was at someone else's house, sleeping on their old couch.

The girl quietly followed Jean into the kitchen, which was the most organized place she had ever seen. The walls were painted yellow. Quartz countertops sparkled in the late afternoon light. Dishes were drying on racks. And more antiques lined the windowsills where the afternoon sun shone through the glass.

There was an island in the middle of the kitchen. On it was a plate with a slice of ham, toasted garlic bread, and half a potato.

Alli's stomach growled noisily as her nose caught a whiff of the buttery bread. She sat down on the stool next to the bar. She picked up a shining fork next to her plate and started to eat. When Alli finished scarfing down her food, she wiped her mouth on the back of her hand. "Thank you, Jean. That was really good," Alli said.

"You're welcome, sweetheart." Jean smiled again. Alli wondered if that was what Jean did half of the day. "Charles and I have to go out to the garden this morning and harvest the peaches that are ripe enough to pick. You could come too," she explained.

"Um, yes," Alli hesitated before continuing. "But my friend and mom are being held hostage by a group called the Order, and I need help finding them. I don't know where they are," she blurted.

"Good. I'll get you some new clothes so you can come help us, and I can wash the ones you're wearing."

Alli scowled. Jean had completely ignored the fact that Essence and her mom were locked up. She would just have to figure out how to save them by herself.

CHAPTER SIXTEEN

The Orchard

After Alli changed into the clothes Jean gave her (a pair of light jeans and a red, button-up shirt), she followed the elderly woman outside toward the farm's orchard. Alli gasped. The trees, the grass, and the flowers weren't dead or in piles of ash. Instead, they were alive.

How? Alli thought to herself. *How had this country farm been spared?*

She spotted an organized garden overflowing with ripe tomatoes, bright green cucumbers, Brussels sprouts, and jalapeno peppers. In a nearby pasture were speckled, muscular plow horses and fat beef cows. A border collie trotted along with Alli and licked her hand. She giggled.

A white fence surrounded the orchard, protecting it from unwanted critters. Fruit trees were in carefully arranged rows, the sun shining through their leaves.

Jean strode straight for the orchard's front gate and opened it, resulting in a deafening shriek that disrupted the quiet glade.

Alli followed, stepping into what felt like another world. The orchard was one of the most beautiful places she had ever seen. There were plum trees planted to the right of the gate and apple trees on the left.

Jean beckoned Alli to follow her. The trees got smaller and smaller the farther they walked from the shrieking gate until they became mere saplings. Soon they turned into young peach trees bearing fuzzy fruit.

At the end of the row, Alli could see the other end of the white fence. Behind it were haunted, dark woods, and Alli made a mental note to never explore past the protective gate.

The border collie squeezed under the fence, barely fitting through. He bounded over to Alli who bent and scratched the playful canine behind his ears. But then she remembered her dog, Jax, back home. The thought filled her chest with loneliness. She missed how he trailed behind her everywhere she went and how he barked when the mailwoman wished Alli good morning as she delivered their mail. But most of all, she missed how Jax curled up next to her at night while she read in bed.

She stopped petting the border collie and continued to follow Jean, stuffing her hands in her pockets and staring at the muddy ground.

"Hon, here we are," said Jean, stooping down to pick up a basket and handing it to Alli. Jean pointed at a tree full of plump, juicy peaches. "We have to pick these today before they get too ripe," she smiled.

Alli strode over to a tree and plucked a peach off its stem where it had previously hung. The fruit was a rosy pink color and had a fuzzy coat lining the outside of it like a warm blanket protecting it from the cold. She smiled again for what seemed like the thousandth time that day.

The girl worked in a daze while plotting a plan to save her friend and mom.

Alli's head snapped up at the grumble of an engine. A wave of dread and panic washed over her like a cold splash of water as she remembered that the Order was still searching for her. She dropped her basket of peaches and started to climb up the tree, hoping its branches hid her enough so she would be able to hide. Then Alli saw a gleaming, red tractor drive through the rows of trees, pulling a giant trailer behind it.

Alli realized the tractor sounded like the flatbed trucks the Order and Night drove around. She chuckled at herself for flipping out and worrying that they had somehow found her at this little farm.

The girl swiftly swung down from the tree and landed on the brittle grass with a soft thud. The gleaming tractor pulled up next to Jean, and a man hopped down from the seat. He was tall and lean, his hands calloused from years of hard work on the farm. He was dressed in a worn-out straw hat and overalls. It was Charles, Jean's husband.

He glanced at Alli, giving her a quick nod before he started picking up the baskets filled with fruit and piling them onto the old trailer.

Alli started picking peaches again, neatly setting them in the fifth basket she had been working on.

"Hon, you can start stacking them on the trailer," Jean yelled from another row of peach trees.

Alli grabbed a basket and padded toward the trailer. "Thanks!" shouted Jean, loading her own heavy basket.

There were probably 15 baskets full of plump, sweet peaches already on the trailer. Alli couldn't even guess what the Hayeses were going to do with all of them. She figured they would either sell them or process the fruit and stick them in the freezer. Alli had absolutely no idea how they could sell them. From what she could tell, there wasn't a supermarket anywhere nearby.

Alli continued to pile baskets of peaches on top of each other until the trailer was stacked so high it looked like they could all tumble down any second. She hoped they wouldn't because they would very likely fall on top of her. It would have been a peach-alanche.

CHAPTER SEVENTEEN

Peach Processing

That night in the kitchen, Alli helped the Hayeses clean, skin, slice, and can the peaches. Jean gave Alli the job of putting the thinly sliced fruit into jars and neatly organizing them in their freezer, which was in the shed outside.

Alli organized the jars in a large basket and hefted them across the yard in the dark. She had forgotten to ask for a flashlight, so she was nervous about going out alone. At one point she was fairly certain she saw a face peek out from behind the orchard's white fence.

She stopped dead in her tracks and stared, her heart skipping a beat. But what she thought she saw was gone without a trace. Alli hurriedly brought the peaches to the barn and put them in the freezer, stacking them into neat columns. The freezer lid dropped with a thud as she sprinted back to the farmhouse as quickly as possible, her skin crawling. She was sure someone was out there.

* * *

When they were done cleaning up from processing the fruit, Jean showed Alli a small guest room in the basement. "We'll bring a space heater down for you since it feels like it's negative 50 in here."

Alli was happy Jean offered because the room was dark and cold. She didn't have any pajamas to change into, so she immediately climbed into the springy bed that was coated with a thin layer of dust. She buried her face into the old, faded pillow and thought about her mom and her friend. She didn't know how she would ever find them. As mad as Alli was at Essence, she hated herself for leaving them.

Another thing that concerned her was the face she had seen. Was someone spying on her? Was it the Order? Was it Night? What if they found her? What would happen then?

She sighed. So many unanswered questions. So many what-ifs.

Alli pulled out the pendant her mom had given her and stared at it. She fingered the charm. It felt like her world was slowly becoming the fantasy stories she always liked to read. The thought made her nervous, and she didn't know what to think about it.

She needed help. Alli needed to find Essence. She had a plan at last; she just needed to find her friend first. To accomplish that, she would have to locate where the Order was, but she had no clue where they were.

With those thoughts—some comforting, others discomforting—she adjusted her pillow and fell asleep before one of the Hayeses had even brought her the heater.

CHAPTER EIGHTEEN

Cyrus

"**N**ow, use your knees to hold tight, and if you have to, grasp the horn with one hand while you use your other to direct the beast."

Charles was teaching Alli how to ride a horse for the first time. She wasn't sure what to think of being so high off the ground and the swaying movement of the horse's walk, but it was best to learn in case she needed the skill one day. It was also something that distracted her from the growing stress of finding her mom and rescuing her. She had been at the Hayeses' little farm for five days, and she still didn't have any idea how to find Essence.

"Ready?" Charles asked. "We're going to go a bit faster." He clicked his tongue at the energized horse, and it sprang into a gallop before Alli had time to react.

She scrambled to find a way to hold on better as the horse galloped past the orchard. Alli finally settled for holding on to its black, brittle mane, wrapping it around her hand. She adjusted how she sat so she was more comfortable. The girl found that riding a horse wasn't so bad after all once you figured out how to do it. The animal swiftly galloped around the farm, neighing and shaking his mane happily.

Alli slowed the horse when she reached the top of a steep hill that overlooked the beautiful glade and the dark forest that lay on the other side. From where she sat perched on the horse, she could see the white farmhouse and the barn.

"Alli! Charles! It's time for dinner!" Jean called from the house, her voice riding on the wind. Alli clicked her tongue, and the horse began to trot down the hill.

Alli enjoyed horseback riding. It was calming. The way the horse swayed when it walked made her want to fall into a deep sleep and forget about all her worries.

She shook her head, reminding herself that she needed to stay focused on finding her friend. That would be her first priority. The only problem with her plan was that she didn't know where Essence was or how to find out where she was. Alli had no way to contact her. And if she did, Alli suspected that Essence was still being monitored closely. It was like a wall that she didn't yet know how to get over.

By this time, Alli had reached the bottom of the hill, and she beckoned the equine into a gallop toward the barn where Charles was patiently waiting for her. She was feeling comfortable on the horse even though she had only been riding 30 minutes.

"Good work, Alli," Charles congratulated her, taking the halter and reins off the horse when Alli dismounted. "Are you sure this is your first time riding?" he asked, looking at Alli for a moment.

"I'm sure," she replied, feeling useless as she stood watching Charles untack the animal. "I grew up riding motorized bikes," she explained. Charles nodded while handing the saddle blanket to her, and she hung it on a peg mounted on the barn wall.

Charles laid the saddle on top of the blanket and hung up the reins. "C'mon," he said. "Let's go eat before Jean gets angry and our food gets cold."

* * *

After lunch, or what Jean insisted on calling dinner even after both Alli and Charles told her it was called lunch, everyone spent the afternoon outside. Jean worked in the large garden she had been nurturing for weeks, and Charles helped Alli learn how to tack one of their new—and Alli's favorite—horses, the black, dappled one. It was not the same older, buck-skinned horse Alli had ridden earlier. Charles explained that this younger, black, dappled horse didn't have a name yet. He asked Alli what she thought would be a good name for him.

"Cyrus," Alli told him after thinking for a moment.

"Why that name?" Charles asked, curious.

"I read a book where there was a character named Cyrus," Alli shrugged. She had no reason why she would name a horse that name. But it seemed to fit, and she liked it.

"I see," Charles looked confused. Alli didn't really answer his question, but he decided to drop it. "So," he moved on, "to tie the saddle, you loop it through here and loop it again and then bring the end through here. Before you tie it off, make sure it's tight around Cyrus' chest. There you go. Now bring it through there, and pull it as hard as you can," Charles instructed, showing Alli where to loop and tie. "Nicely done," he said, clapping Alli on the back.

She smiled and patted Cyrus on his soft, black nose. The horse nickered and nudged her shoulder with his head, leaving drool and slobber all over her jacket. "Cyrus!" Alli made a desperate show of trying to wipe the spit off. But she was sadly unsuccessful.

Charles laughed out loud, which surprised Alli. She had never heard him laugh like that. His sudden outburst made Alli giggle until

Charles stood doubled over in laughter. Finally, he calmed down enough to pat the saddle and say, "Get on up, and ride wherever you want. I trust that you will come back before dinner?"

Alli was surprised that he would let her do this. "Yes, I will." She cocked her head to the side. "Why do you trust me? I've only been here five days."

Charles' face broke into a grin. "I think you have plans that need to be taken care of." He tapped his temple as if he had read Alli's mind.

Alli nodded. She couldn't tell how Mr. Hayes knew she had stuff to take care of, but she assumed she had accidentally said something. She needed to be more careful about when and where she talked to herself. "I'll be back." She clicked at Cyrus, and the obedient horse turned and rode in the direction Alli instructed, his pure black mane billowing in the wind.

CHAPTER NINETEEN

The Face

Alli rode Cyrus into the dark woods. She didn't know why she did, but the woods didn't seem so scary in broad daylight. Besides, woods were just woods. Nothing terrible could happen except getting lost. Another strange thing was that this forest had been spared from the black ash. The undergrowth seemed as healthy as could be.

Her body was jittery with nerves, but she would have to rein in her fear so she wouldn't put fear in Cyrus too. "Positive emotions," Alli told herself. "Right, Cyrus?" she addressed the horse. He walked on through the thicket, offering nothing encouraging.

Alli frowned. "Thanks."

They rode a little farther until the forest became so thick that Alli could no longer ride atop Cyrus. She dismounted and led the horse by his reins.

A stick snapped. Alli jumped. And the eerie, growing silence of the thicket made her skin crawl. She looked at the scene around her and wondered if she was not the only one in the woods.

She continued exploring, more carefully and alert than she was only a minute ago. She still had the growing feeling of being watched.

Leaves rustled loudly, and Alli was sure she was not the only one in the forest. She inspected the landscape around her, taking in every little detail of the forest. Her body was starting to shake from nerves and fear. She knew now that wherever she went there would always be the possibility of the Order or Night finding her.

The trees started to thin out, allowing Alli to heave herself up onto Cyrus again and move much more quickly than before.

Her breath caught when she spotted a dark, hooded face peek out from behind a tree. "Who are you?" Alli yelled, hoping for a response.

The figure raised their eyebrows and then ducked behind the tree again. Alli grunted in annoyance. Couldn't anything go her way?

She immediately scolded herself for that selfish thought. Life was not all about her. She would have to learn that sooner or later.

For the second time on her ride, she dismounted Cryus and carefully approached where the person was hiding. "Hello?" Alli whispered. Cyrus whinnied madly, and Alli spun around like a spinning top, meeting the figures that stood before her.

A boy and a girl in matching black cloaks that brushed the ground stood before her. The boy's look was hard as stone, but the girl smiled a familiar smile and pulled down her hood, revealing a long plait of brown hair. "Hello, Alli."

It was Essence.

CHAPTER TWENTY

Reunited

A rush of anger overwhelmed Alli. Although she was relieved by Essence's appearance, it didn't mean she had forgiven her. "Hello," Alli said plainly. "Have you planned any other kidnappings lately?"

Essence's smile faltered, and she looked like she had just been punched in the gut. She looked hurt and then sad. "I understand why you don't want to forgive me. But there's something I need to tell you." A worry crease formed on her forehead. Her irises were bleak with sleepless nights and didn't show the twinkle that her unique brown eyes normally possessed.

Alli said nothing.

Essence motioned to the boy next to her. "This is Archie, a former Night member. He grew up in it, but like me, he realized what they were trying to do and ran away. But before he did, he gathered information, which explains a *lot*."

Alli looked at the boy, Archie, whose dark features were twisted into a frown. His brown eyes flicked to her for a second before continuing to scan the clearing. He appeared to be about 15.

"You're the face I have been seeing the last couple days," Alli realized.

"Yes." His voice was high-pitched. "We have been watching you," he told her simply.

"Why? How in the world did you find me?"

"Well," said Essence slowly, "we were quite surprised when we did find you here, but it turned out to be a good thing that you were staying right next to us."

"Next to you?" Alli was starting to get tired of being the only one asking all the questions.

"We have a small camp in these same woods. More and more kids keep coming, some from the Order and some from Night. Others are kids who left both organizations a long time ago and have come back to help."

Alli was about to ask, "Help with what?" but she decided she was done asking questions. Instead, she let out a soft "oh" and nodded her head.

Essence could see there was more Alli wanted to ask, but she could also sense a growing annoyance from her friend. "Archie, I think it would be better if we showed her."

Archie nodded. "I agree," and he grabbed Cyrus' reins and started to walk off into the woods.

"Hmm. He seems angry that I'm here," Alli observed.

"He gets suspicious when he meets new people." Essence briskly walked ahead, leaving Alli behind.

CHAPTER TWENTY-ONE

The Hideout in the Trees

A s Alli followed Essence and the boy, she studied the forest. For the first time, she actually saw the beauty of the woods. The trees were bare and covered in a blanket of frost that encased them like a cocoon. The ground crunched with every step, with an occasional snap of a stick and flutter of a startled bird taking flight.

Essence kept ahead of her the whole way to the camp, leaving Alli to walk alone. But the girl didn't mind. Space was good right now. "Whoa!" Alli's eyes widened when she saw where Essence had been hiding out the last few weeks. The trees had grown thicker than the ones in the Hayeses' woods. They were so thick that they were hollowed out in the middle where fires burned inside of them, the smoke billowing upward through the trunk

Archie whistled through his fingers as they came up to a sturdy, wooden platform. A boy with black hair waved at Archie, dropping a rope ladder down in front of him. "Thanks." Archie started up the rope ladder, climbing skillfully until he reached the top, scrambling onto the wooden deck. The platform snaked through the trees and connected to the hollowed-out tree trunks with the fires in them. Where the platforms ended, a handcrafted, shaky rope bridge led to a second platform that connected to another. That occurred a few more times before the decks circled around to meet the one Alli was standing on, forming the shape of a small pentagon.

"Come on, Alli," Essence whispered, her eyes on the ground. "I'll show you around." Essence climbed up the ladder after Archie, with Alli a few rungs behind.

Once on the platform, Alli saw there were many kids her age around her, at least more than 10. Some were skinning dead deer and rabbits, and others were sewing fabric together.

"Here, first I'll show you the extra bedroom we saved for you." Essence led her to a large tree with short, blue tarps attached to the trunk that covered an opening to small individual rooms. There were three doors all the way up the side of the tree and thick branches used to reach the doorways.

Essence climbed up the branches expertly until she reached the middle tarp flap and crawled inside. Alli followed her and was shocked at what she found. The room was only big enough for Alli to curl up in, meaning both girls barely fit in there together. There was a small hole in the middle of the floor and in the ceiling that allowed Alli to look down below her and up above. She gazed around the room and found that it was rather comfortable, even though all that was in it was a pile of deerskins and a blanket sewn together from rabbit fur. It was also *hot*, almost like it was heated somehow.

Then it dawned on her as she looked through the hole in the floor. Sure enough, there was a fire at the bottom of the tree. It was there to heat the small rooms. It was a perfect setup because at night they wouldn't have to struggle with being cold on account of the fall weather.

The walls were roughly carved, and the ceiling was low, probably only three feet high. That meant Alli had to crawl around on her hands and knees.

"You did this?" Alli questioned.

"Well, not me. I prefer hunting. But Archie and all the boys built these. And it's a good thing, too, because it's way better than what we were doing before."

"What's that?"

"Sleeping on the ground." Essence shivered. "It's much safer like this. I would wake up in the middle of the night and see a glowing purple and occasionally blue light float through the fog. It would scare me half to death. It just wasn't safe."

"Hmm." Alli was still in awe at what Essence had been doing that past week while Alli was comfortably hiding at the Hayeses' farm, learning how to ride a horse and preserve peaches when there were more important things she should have been doing.

"C'mon, I'll show you how we get food," Essence suggested before crawling toward the deerskin flap and sweeping it to the side, swiftly descending the branches. Alli clumsily followed her. "So how did you get so many people here?" Alli asked. She was curious why so many kids her age had come here, of all places, and how in the world they had found out about it.

"Most of us here were former Night and Order members. A few grew up in the organizations and then realized what they were doing was wrong and turned against the group. Archie and I opted to rally anyone who wanted to have a real home and stop both the Order and Night, and people came. Some of the kids here are only seven. Take Ruby, for instance. She's probably the most encouraging person we have here. She never gives up on anything. *And* she came up with the idea of the whole group being called the Pentagon since all the platforms together form that shape."

Alli tried really hard to follow along with what Essence was saying, but it was so much information that she felt as if her brain were slowly shutting down.

While Essence was talking, she led Alli over to a shack built into the tree. The trunk was hollowed out like all the others, but this one was tall enough to stand in. The shack had a roof that connected to the trunk of the tree and hung out five feet. There were walls on each side, but the front had a blue tarp for a door. "Come on!" Essence raised the tarp and showed Alli inside. A rank smell filled Alli's nostrils, choking her. She gagged.

Raw meat hung from the ceiling, and a fire blazed in a carefully arranged pit on the floor. "This is the smokehouse," Essence explained. "We cook the food in here overnight until morning when we eat. Then we go hunting and do it all over again until the next day." She paused for a moment, a thoughtful look passing over her features.

"I have something else to show you." She walked out of the smokehouse.

CHAPTER TWENTY-TWO

Disappearance

"This is where we keep all the produce." Essence raised the flap of a second shack. This one was cool and damp on the inside, unlike the heated smokehouse, and shelves lined the walls. Alli peered inside and found that the shelves were filled with all sorts of fresh produce. Carrots, celery, snap peas, plump tomatoes, crispy potatoes, peppers of all different colors, Brussels sprouts, apples, plums, strawberries, avocados, and peaches lined the walls.

There were so . . . many . . . peaches. Baskets of them littered the ground, robbing the shack of floor space. There were peaches in jars, too, and all of them looked oddly familiar to Alli. They looked exactly like the ones she had taken out to the Hayeses' barn freezer. "Wait!" Alli spread her hands out before her. "These baskets look familiar. The jars too." Alli turned and looked her friend in the eyes, suspicious.

Essence nodded. "I was wondering if you would recognize those." She paused for a second. "We have had help, you see. Getting tools and enough wood and food was a challenge for us in the beginning. But Archie met someone who wanted to help. That's how we have built all this already."

"Who?" Alli asked, pressing Essence for answers.

"I think Archie said his name was Charles Hayes."

That confirmed Alli's suspicion. It *was* Charles. *That's* why he let Alli take Cyrus into the woods. *That's* how he knew there were things Alli needed to do.

"I'll be back before sunset," Alli said, looking at the sun and predicting that she had about two hours before nightfall. Essence nodded uncertainly but did not object when Alli raced to the edge of the platform, climbed back down the rope ladder, jumped onto Cyrus, and galloped through the woods back to the Hayeses' home.

* * *

It took Alli longer than she would have liked to return to the Hayeses' farm, but she refused to let that discourage her. She had a lot of questions and wanted every single one of them to be answered.

Alli slowed, leading Cyrus to the front door of the simple, white farmhouse. She dismounted and knocked on the ugly, yellow door that Jean was very fond of.

The door opened, and the elderly woman stared at Alli, her eyes gray and stony with a suspicious but grieving look to them. Alli could tell something was wrong because she had never seen Jean's eyes look like that. "Come in." That seemed to be the only greeting Alli would be getting. Jean stepped aside, and Alli walked in, glancing around the familiar living room and looking for Charles.

"Where's Charles?" Alli slowly turned and fixed her gaze on Jean who looked close to tears. The young girl did a double-take. Jean had never looked so sad, scared, and defeated like she did at that moment. She always had a smile on her face, humming to herself.

Fear knotted inside Alli's stomach. "What happened?" Her eyes locked with Jean's sad ones.

A silent tear trailed down Mrs. Hayes' face. "He's gone. Disappeared." That was all she managed, whimpering.

"When?" Alli asked urgently.

"Right after you left. He had been out in the barn for a while, so I walked out to check on him. As I neared the building, I saw Charles. He was standing in the corner of the horse's stall. When he saw me, he told me to run and hide. He said, 'They've come again,' and then his form became a blur, and he was gone. It felt like something ran past me, but I saw nothing after that." Jean buried her face in her gray and yellow skirt, her body shaking with tears.

Alli nodded. She felt the blood leave her face. "Mrs. Hayes, we have to go." Alli pulled on the old woman's arm, but Jean turned away from her.

"No," she wept. "I'm staying here in case Charles returns." She insisted.

"But Jean, it's not safe. We have to go."

"No!" the woman yelled, pulling away when Alli reached for her a second time.

Alli knew she had lost the battle, and she would have to leave her there. "Okay, Mrs. Hayes. Take care of yourself."

Alli walked out the door.

* * *

Cyrus was being ridden harder than he had ever been ridden before. He could tell something wasn't right. He had heard the wails from his master's wife, and he could sense fear from the girl who was riding atop him. If something really was wrong, then he wanted to make sure his rider was safe, and he wanted to show that he cared even though he didn't know what the problem was.

He galloped through the woods, knowing that Alli wanted to go back to the place they had been earlier. Alli didn't even have to lead Cyrus. He just knew.

The girl was close to tears. Again, more people Alli cared about had disappeared, and she dreaded the thought of losing those people forever. She didn't know how many more people she would have to lose before everyone was safe again. Maybe none of them would be safe. Maybe it would stay like that the rest of her life.

Alli whistled for the rope ladder to be lowered. It dropped, and Alli jumped onto the rungs, climbing up so fast that she lost her grip multiple times.

"Essence! Archie!" Alli called for them when she stood on the platform.

Archie raced out of the smokehouse, twine entangled around his hand. "What's up?" he asked when he got to her.

"I need to talk to you and Essence. Where is she?" Alli asked.

"She went hunting for birds before all of them went south for the winter. Should be back in the next hour," he said casually. "Why are you asking?"

"Charles Hayes is gone. Jean said he disappeared."

Archie's eyes went wide.

"This," he said slowly, "is really bad."

"Why?" Alli desperately spread her hands out before her.

"Because Charles knows where this place is. And Order and Night can coax anything out of anyone."

CHAPTER TWENTY-THREE

Nightwatching

O ver an hour later, Essence returned with the rest of the girls from the Pentagon. Alli personally thought it was an odd name for the hideout, but she wasn't part of it, so it shouldn't matter to her.

How Essence had a knack for hunting Alli didn't know. But she was at least thankful that her friend wasn't starving out here. The girls' catch wasn't as much as they would have liked. It consisted of only a goose and her few eggs, which wouldn't last the Pentagon two days, maybe not even one meal.

"Essence." Alli pushed through the small crowd of girls toward her friend. "I need to talk to you."

Essence had a tired look on her face, but she nodded. Her grey eyes were even duller than they had been before the girls left.

* * *

"Jean said Charles' shape blurred, and then he was gone. But she didn't see anything or anyone else." Alli was sitting with Essence and Archie around a fire that burned in the middle of a deserted platform, listening intently on the opposite side of the hot flames. Both of their faces seemed so tired that Alli felt guilty for dumping all this information on them.

When she insisted on talking to the two of them, they led her to a private platform that was used for gatherings with the Pentagon. That meant they could talk in peace and not worry about anyone eavesdropping.

Night soon fell, and the glow of the warm fire and the chirps of the musical crickets eased Alli's worry. She felt drained, physically and mentally. She longed for her first night in the warm, hollowed-out tree, wrapped up in the rabbit-skin blanket.

"So what do we do now?" Archie asked.

Essence blew out a long breath. "Well, I guess we're gonna have to be more alert and on the watch for anyone from either of the systems. We can position nightwatchers, and we have a bit more lumber left, so maybe we have enough for a couple watchtowers."

Alli and Archie nodded. "Who'll watch tonight, then?" Archie wondered, raising his eyebrows.

"Well," Essence started, looking at them cautiously, "I assume we will, considering we don't want anyone else to know about this yet. Alli, are you good with that?"

Alli realized she wouldn't be getting the sleep she had longed for, but if it meant protecting and keeping others safe, she would gladly do it.

"Yes," Alli said, sitting up straighter. "I'll help."

* * *

Two hours later—after everyone except Archie, Alli, and Essence had gone to bed—the three separately walked around the platforms, each holding a lantern in their hand, making sure they shone them in every shadowy area.

Alli jumped at every sound—the ruffle of a bird's feathers, a hooting owl, a cricket chirping close by, the stir or snore of someone sleeping in their warm room.

She walked to the edge of a platform and looked down at the ground far below that was blanketed in a heavy layer of fog. She was certain she saw a black cloak float through the gloom before it was enveloped by fog. Alli squinted, willing the fog to clear enough to see below her. A red light flashed through the heavy mist, but it disappeared as quickly as it had come. Alli gasped but continued her watch. She couldn't get scared and back down now.

Ten minutes later, Alli heard voices from below her. They were talking hurriedly in hushed whispers. She stared down into the thick gloom. She couldn't see anything, but she still heard the muffled conversation. And now the voices were moving. Quickly, Alli bolted to the rope ladder and lowered it, taking each rung two at a time before she jumped to the ground.

She ran to catch up with the quickly fading voice. A stick snapped to Alli's right, but she couldn't see far through the fog, which meant she was unable to identify what had caused the stick to break. Alli kept running until the voices got closer. Slowing, she crouched, crawling on her hands and knees. Two figures were barely visible through the fog. The first was tall, the second shorter. They appeared to be having a serious conversation.

Alli didn't dare crawl any nearer in case she was spotted. The girl stopped where she was, hidden behind a rock. She was about 10 feet away from the two, but she was close enough to hear tiny snippets of their conversation.

"There," the second said. "I think we're safe now." Alli could tell it was a girl's voice.

"Good call," said the first. She was definitely a grown woman. Her voice was low. "We can't have anyone overhear. Have you stolen the Path yet?" Her voice grew serious.

"No," the second replied. "I'm sorry. I should be trying harder, but it's hard because she still doesn't trust me."

"I know, my daughter, I know."

So, Alli thought, *we're working with a mother and daughter. They're obviously from the Order. But who are they?*

She continued eavesdropping.

"The only problem is that she wears the pendant around her neck. How am I supposed to snag that?" the shorter silhouette argued, spreading her hands out before her. She sounded flustered.

"In time," soothed the first. "Be patient, Essence."

Essence! She was the one under that cloak. She was having a meeting with her mom, Miriam Hunt! And she was planning on stealing Alli's necklace!

The girl held back tears of rage.

Traitor.

The word popped into Alli's head, and she didn't stop it because she knew it was true.

Essence was supposed to be back at the Pentagon watching for the Order, not having secret meetings with them. Technically, Alli was supposed to be there, too, not eavesdropping on a conversation in the middle of the woods. Then again, it was a good thing she had followed because she now knew that Essence was 100 percent untrustworthy. She balled a fist.

"I need you to hurry up with that necklace, my dear. We have to find that last orb and destroy it." Miriam reached through Essence's hood to tenderly stroke the girl's pale cheek. "We can't let anyone go and give away our secret Order. Then everyone would know. Now go. You are supposed to be scouting for me and the rest of the organization. Better get back to it." Miriam smiled before she pulled out her orb and floated away through the forest, leaving a trail of dead plants and wildlife behind, forever scarring the Pentagon's patch of healthy forest.

Alli watched Essence stand silently in the middle of the woods, curious about what she would do. The girl didn't move for two whole minutes. She must have been lost deep in thought.

I need to get back before Essence notices me, Alli thought. She slowly backed away from her hiding place behind the rock, willing herself not to make a sound. When she was 15 feet or so from Essence who was still standing there like a statue, Alli stood and ran back to the camp as fast as her legs would carry her. She had to tell Archie.

The girl all of a sudden heard heavy footfalls behind her. Alli looked back and saw Essence's silhouette, cloak free, running toward her. Alli pumped her legs harder. The fog was so thick that maybe Essence hadn't spotted her yet. Essence couldn't know there had been someone spying on their private conversation.

"Alli," Essence called. Alli ran harder.

"Alli!" she called again. This time, Alli reluctantly slowed down, turning to face Essence, her face twisting into a scowl.

"What?" she asked. "Are you here to apologize for plotting to steal from me? Are you going to finally admit that you really are not on our side?"

"It's . . . complicated." Essence nervously twisted her fingers.

"Really?" Alli scoffed. "It doesn't seem complicated to me. I thought we were friends, Essence. I trusted you! But you have cut a deep gash in our friendship, and I don't think it can be sewn back together." Alli wiped tears from her eyes. Her best friend had betrayed her.

"I know." Essence admitted. "I have made many mistakes. I don't even know why you're still talking to me."

"Well, I'm going to stop. Should I tell everyone about your little conversation?" Alli kicked a tree in anger. Essence's face paled.

"C'mon!" Essence's chin wobbled. "We should get back anyway." Alli noticed she had avoided her question.

The girl nodded before turning on her heel and stalking toward the rope ladder.

* * *

"Find anything?" Archie asked once the three had regrouped.

"Nope. Nothing," said Alli, glaring at Essence.

Essence said nothing. Her shoulders were slouched, and she had dark circles under her eyes. Her irises flicked nervously toward Alli every few seconds. "Dawn's gonna be here in the next hour, which means I'll have to go hunt after breakfast." Essence ran a hand down her tired face. "I'm gonna go to sleep. Everything's good, and the Order wouldn't risk attacking near morning." She stood.

"Same for Night." Archie agreed, nodding his head.

The three of them spoke no more words as they walked back to their rooms. Archie left to go to the boys' platform while Alli and Essence made the way to theirs. Neither spoke, but their expressions and angry or nervous glances said everything. Essence looked like she could pass out from exhaustion, and Alli didn't feel much different. As she wearily climbed up the ladder to get to her room, she swept aside the tarp and crawled into her warm pile of fur blankets, her room nicely heated. The sun peeked over the trees, waking the birds and all the small animals that inhabited the woods. And a new day began.

* * *

"*Alli.*" The voice was calling her again.

"*I'm still waiting,*" the sweet voice spoke in her dreams.

"*Come to me.*"

"*Alli.*"

"*Alli . . .*" the voice faded, softly leaving her dreams. Softly. Softly. Before it was gone.

* * *

Alli woke up some hours later. She sat up as best she could in her den and rubbed the sleep from her eyes. Smoke from the fire at the foot of the tree billowed through the hole in the floor and up into the room above her.

"Hello." Long red hair dropped into Alli's room from above her. Alli looked up, and a toothy grin greeted her. "Who're you?" the girl asked, cocking her head to the side. She was young, no more than seven or eight. She had long, red hair that had to have reached her tiny waist. But at the moment, her hair had fallen through the hole in Alli's ceiling like a fiery, red curtain. The girl had forest green eyes, and a petite face stretched into a welcoming grin.

Alli smiled back. "I'm Alli," she said. "What's your name?"

"Ruby," she replied, surprising Alli by squeezing through the hole and into the tiny room with skill and grace.

Alli nodded, remembering Essence talking about Ruby, something about hunting and coming up with the idea of calling their group the Pentagon.

"Oh, yes. You're good at hunting, right?"

The girl laughed. "Yes," she said. "But my sister Riley is much better than me. And I also have a brother named Ryker. We're triplets." She grinned again.

Alli raised her eyebrows. It isn't every day that you meet triplets. "Hmm" was all she had to give in response.

The small girl didn't seem to mind. "C'mon, I'm hungry. I'll show you where we eat."

CHAPTER TWENTY-FOUR

The Meeting

A rchie was busy building watchtowers that sat nested in the tops of the large trees. They would overlook the whole fortress, perfect for spotting anything suspicious. Really, the towers were just a plank large enough for someone to sit on or stand on. They were unable to make them too fancy because of their growing lack of wood.

He heard the rustle of leaves below him and looked down from where he was, desperately hugging the tree. He had been trying to drive a nail into a fat branch that would serve as the platform's support, but the nail just would not cooperate.

"Oh hey, Alli." He dropped his hammer onto the unfastened two-by-four and swiftly swung down 40 feet from where he had been perched, landing softly on the ground to meet the girl.

"What are you doing around here?" asked Archie, swinging his hand in a wide arc.

"Taking a walk, I guess. Had some things on my mind I needed to think through."

"Oh," Archie replied. "Are you having trust issues with Essence?" He raised an eyebrow knowingly.

"Yeah . . . Wait. How did you know?" Alli asked, her heartbeat picking up speed.

"Well, not to be nosy or anything, but every time I walk by you, you're muttering something about how Essence is untrustworthy, not to mention the angry side-eyes you give every time you see her."

Alli lowered her gaze to the ground. "I know I should forgive her, but she helped plan my mother's kidnapping. And when we were supposed to be watching for the Order last night, she was having a meeting with her mother in these very woods. So I really don't know what to think."

Archie nodded his head. "I know. Essence told me everything. She's in a hard place right now. She wants to stop the Order, but it's her mother she's dealing with. So she's torn between what's the right thing to do and what it looks like to obey Miriam. Alli, honestly the best thing I can say to fix this mess is to go and talk to her. Figure out what's really going on in there." He tapped his temple.

Alli nodded and sighed. "All right. I'll go talk to her."

Archie smiled. "It'll be worth it," he said.

"I hope so." Alli walked back toward the camp.

* * *

Alli met Essence at the hideout's rope ladder. Essence was just about to scurry up the rungs when Alli called to her.

"I thought you weren't talking to me," Essence reminded Alli, raising her eyebrows.

"I know. But I want to know the whole story, like why you helped kidnap my mom. And why were you trying to steal the necklace from me?"

Essence sighed. "Look, I know you're just going to chew me out again. So just leave me alone, okay?" She started to climb up the ladder.

Alli rushed forward and grabbed Essence's wrist. "Wait! Please, Essence," Alli pleaded. "I'm just trying to make things right again."

Essence sighed again. "Okay." The girl climbed back down the ladder, although Alli could tell she was reluctant.

She led Alli over to a wide flat rock next to a stream. The rock was warm from the sun, and the stream trickled and danced playfully. The girls sat down across from each other. Essence stared at Alli. "What do you want to know?"

"Well," Alli started, "my first question is obviously this: Why did you kidnap Mom?"

Essence lowered her eyes. "My mother wanted the pendant. She never told anyone why, only that she would get it one day. She always said she needed it and that your mom didn't have the right to keep it. So I'm assuming that's why she kidnapped your mom. It was all so she could get the pendant."

"But why did you agree to distract me?" Alli asked.

"Because . . . I knew you wouldn't be harmed if I did. I wouldn't have let you touch that orb—ever. And I made myself promise I would keep your mom safe at all costs."

Alli nodded before she continued. "But what about the necklace? Why were you going to steal it?"

Essence rolled her eyes. "I wasn't actually going to steal it. I was just saying that so the Order would think I was still on their side." She locked eyes with Alli. "You *do* know that I really am on your side, right?"

Alli didn't respond. She wanted to believe that Essence truly was on her side, but the same thought always came to mind. *Is she really?*

Essence sighed. "I know I haven't proved completely trustworthy, but please give me a chance."

Alli looked Essence straight in the eye. "I'm trying to, Essence. Honest. I . . . I just need more time."

Essence nodded. "Okay."

* * *

Night came faster than Alli liked. It didn't help that she had slept in until noon. But here she was, gathered around the campfire on the meeting deck with all the kids from the Pentagon.

The group that had left to collect information from the evacuation center had come back that night in time for the meeting. They all looked tired and hungry, especially a girl named Sisuca Barkridge. The girl ran a hand across her dark features, a worn look on her brow.

"Everyone, please listen!" Essence shouted at the small crowd, raising her hands for silence. The triplets stood on her right side, looking up at her with respect. Alli noticed that each of the siblings had green eyes and vibrant, red hair. Riley's hair was not as long as Ruby's, but she made up for it with her tight ringlets, which barely fell past her shoulders. Ryker's hair was short and curly. He had a protective demeanor about him.

Alli watched the siblings with interest, and though they were only seven, they seemed like they knew exactly what was going on, maybe even more than what Alli knew.

Essence looked at Ryker and raised her eyebrows. The young boy nodded, sticking two fingers in his mouth and delivering an ear-splitting whistle.

"Thank you," Essence said when everyone became quiet. "So the team we sent to collect information came back today, which was perfect timing for our meeting. Sisuca informed me that they have collected important information that could explain most everything, like why our own patch of forest hasn't turned to ash yet."

Alli frowned. She had to admit that was something she had been wondering about since she arrived at the Hayeses' farm. "Sisuca thinks she and her team may have figured out why, which would be helpful since this has been something that has clouded everyone's minds and thoughts." Essence waved her hand, beckoning Sisuca to come forward.

Sisuca—despite her tired features—had an excited gleam in her eye as she stepped up in front of everyone. "Yes, but before we get to that, we have something much more important to tell you. We have all known what the orbs are, but we were not quite sure what they did. For the longest time we had theorized they were teleporters since Miriam Hunt had never specified their purpose. We found that they take us to another dimension—a darker dimension—which is where we think the Order and Night dwell, and that is why they are so dangerous. We are in that dimension now.

"This place is like the flip-side of Earth. The Order and Night have just recently figured out how to get into the real world, but they don't know how to find it. Corrado will show you the answer." She stepped back from the middle of the platform.

A boy with straw-colored hair moved forward, pulling a folded piece of paper out of his coat pocket. The drawing showed another orb, but this one was white and gold with unreadable symbols carved into the face of the sphere.

The crowd gasped, and a murmur of excitement rose through the gathering of kids. But Sisuca raised her hand haltingly. "Before everyone gets excited, there is one problem. We don't have the key to finding it."

The boy, Corrado, pulled out a crude, hurried drawing of a necklace that looked oddly familiar, though Alli couldn't remember where she had seen it.

"This is called the Path. Without this, we cannot find the golden orb, and if we can't find the orb, we can't get back home."

Alli suddenly realized where she had seen the necklace before. It was the one her mom had given her.

CHAPTER TWENTY-FIVE

The Path

"I know where the Path is." Alli spoke above the loud groans of the crowd.

Sisuca stared at her with a look of confusion. "H-how?"

"Well," Alli said cautiously, "I just do."

Archie glanced at her, a frown creasing his forehead. "Then where is it?" he asked, confusion spreading across his face.

Alli glanced at Essence, who nodded her head. She understood what Alli was talking about. Alli smiled at her friend before she turned back to the crowd.

"Right here." She pulled the pendant out from under her shirt, showing it to everyone.

"How'd you get it?" Corrado asked, suspicion clouding his features.

"My mother gave it to me when Miriam Hunt locked us in the same room. My mom said I would need it one day."

"Well, it's a good thing you have it, then." Archie smiled, hope spreading across his face.

"I always believed we would get away from this place one day." Ruby took her siblings' hands, grinning from ear to ear.

A majority of the crowd murmured in agreement. "We're going home at last!" someone cheered from the back of the group.

"Guys! We can't get ahead of ourselves. We still have to find the orb," the boy Corrado said.

The hopeful cheers receded, and Alli was slowly becoming more and more discouraged. She really wanted to get home. She wanted life to become normal again. Everything just wasn't happening fast enough.

"Sisuca, do you know how to find the orb?" Alli asked, staring into the girl's dark eyes.

"No," she said, her shoulders slumped.

"So we don't know how the pendant works?" someone asked with a thick, Southern accent.

"Kind of. It should work like a compass, turning hot when pointed in the right direction," said Alli, remembering the dream she had when the necklace burned her skin. She really hoped the necklace would pulse instead.

"What?" Essence asked. "How do you know?"

"I had a dream. Essence and I were running through a dark tunnel, fighting to get to the end. I was wearing the pendant. It burned like fire." Alli stared into space.

No one seemed to know what to say to that.

"Okay," Essence said carefully. "Well, if you can figure out how to get the pendant to work, that would be great. I believe you can do it."

Alli nodded, thankful that her friend trusted her.

* * *

She lay in bed that night holding the small necklace in her hand, studying it. It was simple, really. It seemed to be made of some sort of metal shaped into a flat circle with the Roman numeral VII carved into it.

And that was all it was—a black circle on a fancy chain.

She traced her finger across the smooth surface of the charm, quickly starting to feel frustrated. Why wasn't it doing anything? She was so close to getting back home, and this tiny necklace was what stood in her way. Everyone was depending on her.

Alli threw the chain across her room and turned her back to where it lay on the floor. She buried her head in her fur blanket and angrily lay there until she fell asleep.

But what Alli didn't know is that after she had fallen into a deep sleep, the pendant started to pulse with a faint glow, beating in the same rhythm as her heart—slow and steady, over and over.

* * *

Thunder cracked again and again. The trees shook. Screams filled the air. Alli jolted awake, scrambling to sweep aside the tarp flap to see what was going on.

Lightning flashed through the sky, first purple and then red, green, yellow, blue, pink, orange, grey, and cyan—and finally, the darkest color, black, which was the thickest bolt of all.

"Alli!" Essence was down below, wading through the crowd of kids. Alli spotted the girl and shimmied down the tree in a hurry. She jumped the last few feet and landed with a *thump* on the deck.

"Essence!" Alli raised a hand and waved frantically, her blonde hair whipping around her face. "Right here!"

Essence ran toward her before skidding to a stop, her face twisted into an expression of worry and fear. "They're here!" she said.

"What's happening?" Alli asked frantically, brushing her wild hair out of her face. The wind had picked up to a high speed, and it was becoming hard for Alli to stand in one spot.

"The Order. And this time Night has come with them!" Essence whispered.

Alli felt the blood drain from her face. "How did they find us?" she gulped.

Guilty tears trailed down Essence's face. "The meeting I had with Mom! She must have seen where we were. I'm so stupid!" She hid her face in her hands.

"Hey!" Alli yelled over the roaring wind. She waited for Essence to look at her. "I know you didn't mean for any of this to happen."

Wiping the tears off her cheeks, Essence gave a small, confident smile. "Let's go meet them, then. Together." Her tone was pure determination.

CHAPTER TWENTY-SIX

Betrayal

Everyone was awake by this time. And all stood at the edge of the platform nearest to the lightning storm, knowing that both organizations would march out of the forest at any moment, each enfolded in dark cloaks.

Alli could tell everyone was on edge, even the triplets. Young as they were, they understood the seriousness of the situation. Essence stood at the head of the group, flanked by Alli and Archie. The girl nervously twirled a strand of hair around her finger.

They stood in eerie silence. Watching. Waiting.

Alli scanned the woods, watching every shadowy area. Her breath caught when she saw the plant life start to blacken before turning to ash. They were close. Very close. Alli watched as everyone, like her, tensed, preparing for what was to come.

Balls of light appeared near the floor of the forest, shining all different colors. And the sphere leading the rest was magenta. Miriam Hunt had arrived.

"Alli!" a voice called confidently. Alli recognized the voice of Mrs. Hunt. "I am here to repossess the pendant as it is not rightfully yours. Also, I am here to take Essence back home."

Alli heard Essence scoff. Her friend shook her head disapprovingly. The girl crossed her arms.

"No. I refuse to go back with you. And the pendant is not rightfully yours. It is Alli's." Essence took Alli's hand and pulled her forward.

Miriam laughed and stepped out of the shadows, the rest of the floating orbs doing the same, revealing their dark, cloaked owners. There were at least 40 of them in all. Alli couldn't help but shiver. There were so many. Not all of them had orbs, but if the people who *did* have orbs wanted to, they could suck up every kid there and hold them hostage.

"I'm sorry, my daughter, but I'm afraid you don't really have a choice," Miriam said coldly.

Essence opened her mouth to object, but before she could, Alli asked, "What do you want, Miriam? Why are you here in the middle of the night?"

"Oh." Miriam lowered her hood, revealing her cold features. "I thought I made that clear. I have come to take the necklace, to claim it as my own as it should have been 14 years ago."

Fourteen years ago? Alli thought. *What happened then?*

"What happened 14 years ago?" Alli asked, trying not to sound *too* interested.

"That is a matter for another time. Besides, it's not all that important."

The crowd gasped, and Alli turned around. Somehow, two black-cloaked members had sneaked onto the platforms behind the kids. The two men pushed aside the older kids—the smaller children being only the triplets—and advanced on Alli, Archie, and Essence.

Archie bravely stepped forward, planting his feet. "Stop right there!" he commanded. The bigger figure chuckled before pushing Archie out of the way. The boy stumbled and fell on his rump, both shocked and annoyed that someone had succeeded in shoving him. Suddenly, both men rushed forward, each grabbing one of Alli's arms. She grunted and struggled but to no avail.

The two men turned her around to face the Order and Night down below. Alli felt like she was being put on display standing this high up. Miriam floated off the ground and glided forward until she was just an arm's length away. Miriam's chestnut hair swirled around her face. She stared at the pendant around Alli's neck, the charm resting just above Alli's collarbone.

"There it is." Miriam's eyes became dreamy. She reached for the charm. Alli struggled with all her might, but the two men held her in place.

"Stay still, young lady," said the first hooded figure. Alli realized the figure's male voice sounded familiar somehow. She just couldn't put a finger on it.

The necklace started to warm, the metal getting hotter the closer Miriam's fingers got to the Path. Mrs. Hunt didn't seem to notice when Alli started tearing up from the burning pain she was experiencing.

Miriam finally made contact with the charm, and Alli screamed as the burn intensified. It took the girl a moment to realize she was not the only one being burned. Miriam had collapsed on the spot and was cradling her hand. She lay on the platform, crying out in agony. The smaller Night member rushed to help his mistress, but there was nothing he could do.

And then all at once, Miriam stopped. She lay there, gasping for breath. After a minute or two, she stood, leaning on the second man. Alli noticed that Miriam had slid her hand into the folds of her cloak.

"Mr. Hayes, we are done here. Essence can do what she likes. I don't care anymore. But that necklace." She pointed at the charm with her good hand. "It's cursed," she declared.

She then turned to float back to the ground when the Pentagon residents gasped. Alli swung around to face them before her jaw dropped. Archie had snuck up behind the first man and pulled down his hood, revealing his features.

She gasped.

Alli knew his voice had sounded familiar. She remembered Miriam calling the man Mr. Hayes. Why hadn't she caught it before?

It was Charles Hayes from the farm, Jean's husband. He was part of the Night organization.

Alli was already filled to the brim with rage and hurt from the last few weeks. Now it all exploded. She shook her head disapprovingly. "How could you?" Tears pooled in her eyes, but she willed them away.

Charles' face remained expressionless. "It was for a good cause." He stared at the pendant around her neck.

Alli pursed her lips and looked down at the necklace where her skin was red and raw from the burn. *This tiny article has caused so much conflict*, Alli thought.

She fingered the charm absentmindedly, still looking at the necklace, and said, "Did you know Jean cried when you left? I went back to see you, and you were gone. I knew either the Order or Night had taken you, so I tried to take Jean back with me. But she wouldn't go. Do you wanna know why?" Alli's voice cracked.

Charles hesitated a moment before nodding. His eyes were full of emotion.

"She was waiting for you to come back home. And she's still there as far as I know. But you left her all alone, wondering if you would ever return."

Charles didn't say anything. He pulled out an orb of his own—a fiery, orange color— and floated off the platform to rejoin the other

Night members. Alli didn't know his reason for joining the dark side, but it wasn't a good one.

"Well, as touching as that was," Miriam concluded, cackling, "it's time for us to go."

Miriam pulled out her orb once again from the folds of her robe and whispered into it. The rest down below did the same. Lightning of all colors flashed. Alli closed her eyes tightly, and when she opened them again, the figures were gone, leaving behind a decaying patch of forest.

CHAPTER TWENTY-SEVEN

A Change of Heart

M iriam Hunt spent most of the next day and part of the night pacing around in her bleached room, lost in thought. Her room was all white, including the bed sheets and frame. She hated that color. It was overwhelming, and it reminded her of sleeping in a hospital room.

The same question kept swirling around in her head. *Why have I taken this path of greed and hate and anger?* She didn't quite know the answer. And that's why she was bothered.

Tired of pacing around her pearly room, she threw open her door, not caring if she disrupted the other sleeping people around her, and marched into the hallway.

It was near midnight, and the moon shone brightly, illuminating Miriam's path as she left the underground building and stormed into the woods. She needed to get away from that place. She had liked the old factory better. It was more spacious.

Miriam sat down by a burbling brook that glided across small pebbles at the bottom, gleaming in the moonlight. The woods were peaceful, and it seemed like they were singing to her, the dark cedar branches swaying in the wind. It was like they were dancing. A woodpecker drummed on a tree in the distance, and an owl hooted a sweet lullaby.

She glanced down at her hand wrapped in cloth that covered the raw, reddened flesh beneath. The skin was still tender, but the burn was gone. She basically traveled to her daughter's hideout just to humiliate herself by screaming her head off like a child. Now people must think of her as a joke. She suspected she would never be taken seriously again.

Miriam sat back and relaxed, the warm night air soothing her tense muscles. An owl hooted and flew overhead, its sleek, white feathers shining like a star. A mouse scurried out from inside a rotten log and paused to stare at Miriam with a beady black eye.

For the first time in years, Miriam Hunt's eyes shone joyfully in the moonlight, and she smiled, feeling at peace with herself. The nagging emotion she had ignored these past weeks exploded inside her. She had caged them in for so long, and now she was letting them go.

Miriam Hunt wasn't going to be with the Order anymore. She was done with that. She felt guilty for causing so much pain to people, especially her daughter. Miriam was ready to change, which meant she had much to do in the meantime.

She would start with Amira Cormac.

* * *

Essence, Archie, Alli, the triplets, Sisuca, and the rest of the Pentagon residents were preparing for the journey ahead of them. All 13 kids in the group seemed to be fueled by the possibility of something new, and all seemed to forget last night's event, which was perfectly fine. Personally, Alli was thrilled she had the chance to go back home.

"Alli!" Sisuca waved her over.

"What's up?" Alli asked, jogging toward the tall, dark-headed figure. The girl had a weary look about her. Alli could tell she was exhausted.

I think last night rattled basically everyone, she thought.

Sisuca flipped a long braid over her shoulder. "I just wanted to thank you. We have been waiting for a way to get home, and when it seemed the team and I had found it, we had only one obstacle. Do you know what it was?" she asked, but she didn't wait for an answer. "The necklace. We didn't know where it was. We hadn't even heard of it before. But you had it. And now the journey should be easy. Did you figure out how the pendant works?"

Alli recalled throwing it across the room last night before she fell asleep. "No. I tried."

Sisuca's reaction made Alli wish she had lied. "Oh." Sisuca turned away from Alli and grabbed a duffle bag, shoving food into it. She was already preparing for the trip.

Alli sighed, pulling the necklace out of her pocket and setting it into the palm of her hand. "Here, Sisuca. You try." She extended her arm.

Sisuca sniffed and turned, tenderly picking up the smooth charm. Cradling it in her hand, she studied it. Sisuca's blank expression turned to a deep frown. "It's getting super warm, almost hot," she stated.

Alli cocked her head. "What?" she asked.

"Ow! It's burning me!" Sisuca flipped her hand over, and the necklace dropped to the wooden platform. Alli reached down to pick it up, muscling through the intense burn of the round charm. Bravely, she pulled the silver chain around her neck and fastened it at the back, the charm resting just above her collarbone.

Alli fingered the charm. She turned slowly. *What if . . .*
Her thoughts trailed off.

"What . . . are you doing?" Sisuca asked, staring at Alli like she had gone mad. She tenderly cradled her burnt hand.

"Testing something."

Alli continued to rotate until the charm started to hum against her skin. Once she faced north, the necklace started to pulse.

CHAPTER TWENTY-EIGHT

North

Everyone was re-energized with Alli and Sisuca's discovery. Alli still couldn't quite believe it had been that easy to find which way they had to travel. The journey sounded pretty straightforward. Alli could tell that everyone, like her, was hoping it would be easy.

She had only spent four days at the hideout, and it already felt like home, other than the fact that she still didn't have her mom with her. She wouldn't go home without her mother. Alli would stay, no matter how bad this place was.

"Alli, we're ready," Archie said, walking up behind her.

"I gotta do something first." Alli turned and faced Archie. "Just real quick."

"What do you have to do?" he pressed.

"My mom is still at the evacuation center. I don't want to leave without her," Alli said with determination. She stuffed her hands in her sweatshirt pocket.

"Then I'll help you." Essence appeared behind Archie, her face shining with excitement. "We have to leave soon, but if we get there and back in the matter of an hour, we should be good."

Alli nodded, thankful she had people who were willing to stand by her side.

The small group climbed down the rope ladder and ran toward the evacuation center, hoping they had enough time to get Mrs. Cormac out before everyone left without them.

Archie led the way until he abruptly stopped in the middle of the narrow deer trail they were following. "Wait," he whispered. "Who's that?"

Essence peeked around him and gasped. Miriam Hunt was walking toward them, balancing a coughing, limping figure. "Mom? Mrs. Cormac?" Essence ran to her mother, concerned by the coughing state of Alli's mom.

Miriam surprised Essence with a tight hug, shifting Mrs. Cormac's weight so the mother could wrap one arm around her daughter. "Essence, I'm so sorry. I never meant to hurt you." Miriam pulled back from Essence, tears pooling in her eyes. "Will you forgive me?"

Essence took her mom's hand in her own. "Mom, I have hoped since the day I left that you would come to our side. Now you have." She hugged her mom one more time before she turned to Mrs. Cormac, pressing her hand against the sick woman's forehead. "Alli, she has a really high fever. Her skin feels like it's burning up."

"Oh!" Alli rushed forward, putting her arm around her mom's shoulders and letting her mother lean on her. Miriam kept one arm around Alli's mom, refusing to let Alli carry her alone. They shared Mrs. Cormac's weight between them.

"We gotta go, or the rest of the kids will leave us behind." Archie reminded them, hooking his thumb toward the hideout.

Alli nodded as both she and Miriam helped Amira Cormac limp toward camp.

* * *

When the group came back to the hideout, 11 kids were patiently waiting for them, everyone carrying their own pack of food and supplies. Sisuca stepped forward, handing Alli, Essence, and Archie their own bags.

"Thank you," Alli said. "We were worried you all would leave without us."

"But we couldn't do that, could we?" Sisuca raised her eyebrows knowingly. "You're the one with the necklace." She grinned.

"True." Alli had forgotten that small detail.

Essence stepped forward. "All right, everyone. It's time to leave," she yelled to the crowd. "We don't exactly know how far this necklace is going to take us, but I will go as far as we have to if that means we can get out of this dark place and make it back home."

"Are we bringing her with us?" one kid shouted. Alli whipped her head toward him. The boy's pale features were twisted into a scowl, his blue eyes flashing with mistrust. "She has to prove we can trust her."

Essence stepped forward and opened her mouth to speak. But before she could say anything, Miriam cut her daughter off.

"This is why you can trust me." She reached into the folds of her cloak, pulled out shards of clear glass, and held them up for all to see. The small crowd gasped, and Alli watched as Essence's jaw dropped in amazement.

The boy stared at the glass, which reflected in the sunlight. Alli's mouth hung open. It was the magenta orb. She had smashed it.

He nodded approvingly, though he still looked reluctant to believe her. "Okay, Mrs. Hunt. We'll see what happens." With that, he turned on his heel and marched to the back of the crowd.

"Who was that?" Alli whispered to Essence.

"Rafael," she said simply. Essence turned to address the crowd. "Let's go," she announced. Miriam smiled, shifting Mrs. Cormac's weight to use her free arm to envelope her daughter in a side hug. Alli stepped toward her mom and wrapped Mrs. Cormac in a tight embrace.

A loud cheer rose from the throng of the small gathering, and everyone turned and marched north, excited to start a new chapter of their life.

CHAPTER TWENTY-NINE

The Journey

After the group journeyed six hours through the forest in warm sunshine, it started to rain again. Alli shivered in her soaked clothes.

People were slipping on the muddy ground, and Mrs. Cormac, who was being guided by Miriam, was coughing even more now that she was struggling to stay warm.

"Mrs. Hunt, let me carry my mom, please. You don't have to do this yourself," Alli begged as she joined the two.

"No," Miriam answered firmly. "I will carry her the whole way." Her voice was full of determination.

"Okay, well, if you need help, let me know."

"I won't."

Alli didn't know if Miriam meant she wouldn't need help or she wouldn't let Alli know if she needed help. She shrugged and caught up to where Essence and Sisuca were walking together. "Hey," Alli said.

"Hey," Sisuca echoed her greeting, wrapping her thin flannel around her body. "How's your mom?"

"Fine. She still has a raging fever, but she's tough," Alli responded, trying to convince herself that her mother would recover. She looked at the girl. "Sisuca, you've never talked about your parents before. What happened to them?"

"I don't talk about them because I have no idea where they are or who they are. I was separated from them when I was young, so I don't remember them. That's what happened to most of the kids here, too, I think," she said briefly.

Alli frowned. "I'm sorry," she said.

"Don't be. This is the only life I have ever known. I'm not even completely sure I'm ready for what's to come."

"You will be," Alli assured her.

"Sure." Sisuca turned to walk with another short-haired girl who smiled at Sisuca encouragingly.

* * *

Everyone traveled in silence, the only sound being the splash and squish of feet meeting the soggy ground. They all shivered from the cold, and Alli's teeth chattered. Why did it have to rain on the day they started their journey?

There wasn't much to talk about while they trekked through the thick forest. The necklace hadn't pulsed or burned since they started their travel. It just hung helplessly around Alli's neck—doing nothing.

She shivered as a gust of wind tore through her sweatshirt. Alli pulled her hood up around her head. Hopefully, the chilling rain would stop soon.

Darkness was drawing near, the sun slowly disappearing below the horizon. Alli didn't know if they were going to stop for the night or keep going. She hoped they would keep traveling because they would be far warmer while continually moving instead of sitting down and freezing all night with no way to start a fire.

Alli decided to follow behind everyone to make sure they didn't leave someone behind. She counted heads. There were 15 in all, including her. Hopefully, none of the kids got lost.

The girl switched her attention to the forest, studying the trees around her. Somehow, they were both beautiful and haunting at the same time. They seemed to be hiding something—something dark. But it couldn't be that. The trees and plant life were green and healthy, not black and ashy.

Alli jumped at the snap of a branch. She spun toward the noise, but the forest was so thick that it hid what lurked in the darkness. Alli kept walking, but she made sure she was aware of her surroundings.

A red light flashed through the bushes on Alli's right. She frowned. There was definitely something strange going on.

She crept toward where the light had been, but there was nothing. Whatever had been there was gone.

Then all of a sudden, the trees and greenery started to turn black. Five dark-cloaked figures melted out of the forest. Three of them held orbs.

The figure in front marched toward Alli with purpose. In their hands was a black orb. Alli immediately knew who was hidden behind the cloak.

"LeRouge." Alli planted her feet, clenching her fists.

LeRouge laughed. "Oh, you're so pathetic." She stopped and lowered her hood. "No need to put on the brave act, sweetie. We haven't come to destroy you and your little friends," LeRouge said matter of factly. She scowled, the scars on her face wrinkling.

"I have come to make a bargain with you and only you," she continued. "That means you would do well not to tell anyone about our little chat." LeRouge's eyes narrowed.

Alli nodded.

"Good. Now, here is my proposition. You take everyone to the last orb, but instead of going back into the real world, you destroy the orb, and we will let you live. If you don't agree to my deal, I will kill all of you. Or if you refuse, I will *still* kill you. What do you say?" she asked.

This is no kind of deal, Alli thought, panicking. *This is a threat. I don't see any way out of it.*

Alli's thoughts raced, but she could find no solution. She reluctantly nodded. She had to protect her friends.

What have I done? Alli asked herself.

LeRouge clapped her hands. "Splendid! Don't worry. This world isn't that bad. It has its rough edges, but no matter. Your family and friends will be spared, I promise. But beware. We are watching you. And know that I won't trust you for a minute."

She sauntered back into the woods, the other Order and Night members following in her wake. After a few minutes, all that was left were rotten logs.

Alli glanced at the path through the forest. The Pentagon had disappeared, leaving her behind.

Alli glanced back at the dead forest, remembering LeRouge's cold tone. The woman scared Alli. Something about her was just terrifying. She shivered and ran to catch up with the rest.

* * *

"Essence, we have to keep walking," Alli told her when they caught up with the group. "We can't stop tonight. It'll be cold, and we don't have a way to start a fire."

"I agree. But I'm worried others won't. They're already tired." Essence sidestepped a large puddle.

"I'm tired, too, but it's better to keep moving than to stop and end up freezing to death in the middle of the night." *And I don't want to meet the Order again*, Alli finished in her head.

"Okay, I'll tell them." Essence turned to address the Pentagon. "Everyone, listen up. We're gonna keep moving north instead of stopping for the night." The travelers groaned. "I know that may not sound like fun to you, but we have to keep pushing forward. It's gonna be okay. We can do this."

So everyone followed Essence. They were tired, wet, and hungry. Their feet were sore, their legs were aching, and they were crying out in protest. Some even thought of turning and going back to the hideout.

Ruby was practically dragging along her sister who fought to go back to the warm shelter of the Pentagon. Ryker was trudging along gloomily behind his sisters, hands in his pockets, his shoulders shaking from the cold.

Ruby's face was desperate, her eyebrows crinkled together. Alli walked clumsily toward the triplets, slipping on wet leaves and stomping through thick, squishy mud. "Here." Alli bent down and beckoned for Riley to wrap her thin arms around Alli's shoulders. The small girl was hesitant, glancing at her sister. Ruby nodded vigorously, and Riley climbed onto Alli's back.

Alli stood, trying not to slip in the mud, and followed after everyone who had passed her. Ruby slipped her delicate, cold hand into Alli's, squeezing it tightly. Alli smiled at her, and the small girl encouragingly smiled back. Riley gently rested her small head on Alli's shoulder and soon, despite the cold rain, fell asleep.

Ruby led them on. She seemed to never grow tired of walking, never grow tired of slipping and falling in the mud, picking herself back up again and leading Alli on.

Alli decided that out of all of them, little, sweet Ruby was the toughest of them all.

CHAPTER THIRTY

The Creek

Night air sliced through the overhang of trees, whipping through everyone's coats and jackets, chilling people to the bone. The sun had disappeared long ago, and there was no moon to light their path.

The rain had finally ceased, leaving behind muddy ground and dripping trees. Alli shivered for the hundredth time. She craved warmth, but there was only the whipping, freezing night air.

All of a sudden, she felt the pendant start to warm against her skin, and a faint pounding filled her ears. Like it had that morning, the necklace began to pulse, growing hotter by the second but not hot enough to burn her numb skin.

The warmth eased her muscles, and her body could finally loosen up. Her muscles had been sore from staying tense for so long, but now she relaxed.

Up ahead, someone stopped and moaned. "There's a deep creek up here. There's no way I'm crossing *that*."

Alli forged ahead, still carrying a softly snoring Riley on her back. "What do you mean?" Alli stopped next to Archie where he had stopped at the rocky bank. Creek was an understatement. River would have been a more fitting description. It was at least 10 feet wide.

Alli looked down into the water where a strong current swirled through the froth. "Archie, how cold is it?"

Archie reached down and stuck the tips of his fingers into the water. "Cold," he said gloomily. He started to wade into the water until the current swept around his knees. "I'm going to cross, though. I'm not going to give up." Determination was etched across his face.

Guilt churned in the pit of Alli's stomach. Why had she agreed to LeRouge's proposition? She obviously wasn't going to destroy the last orb unless she had no other choice. But what if she had to in order to save her friends? Then what? This journey would be for nothing. She squeezed her eyes shut. "I'll figure this out," she muttered to herself.

"What?" Archie asked, glancing at her questioningly.

The girl shook her head. "Nothing."

Ruby offered Alli a small smile before she courageously waded in after Archie. "Same for me," she squeaked, her lips already starting to turn blue. Essence followed in after her, and then went Kaimen, Ryker, and Mrs. Hunt, staggering from Mrs. Cormac's weight. "I'm going too," she said, "and I'm taking Amira with me."

Alli was happy to know that Miriam cared for her mom enough to even try to cross the swirling water with extra weight. "Thank you," Alli whispered gratefully.

The woman nodded, turning around. "So? What are you all waiting for?" Miriam yelled at the older kids in the crowd since the youngest of them were the triplets. "Are you coming or not?" She turned and waded into the water, not waiting for an answer.

Ryker followed behind his sister, Alli wading in after him. Riley was still clinging to Alli's back. The small girl woke with a start when the icy water soaked through her boots. She let out a surprised gasp.

"Hang on, Riley," Alli soothed, steadying herself from the whipping current.

Essence, who was already waist deep in the water, looked back at the remaining people. "Are you guys coming?" Essence raised her eyebrows. Sisuca hadn't even crossed yet.

"Um," Corrado said, stepping forward thoughtfully. "Yes, I'll come," he declared, followed by Kaimen.

"Good," Essence nodded, satisfied that at least someone else would also cross the river. She turned back to the other kids who stood awkwardly, shuffling their feet and avoiding her gaze.

"We're not coming," someone mumbled. "This is more than we thought we were getting into. First, it was raining for hours, and then we didn't get to rest for the night. Now it's crossing a *river*. We'll freeze to death before we even make it to wherever we're trying to go."

"Jakob, you have to keep fighting. All of you. Rafael?" Essence turned toward the boy.

He shook his head. So did everyone else who hadn't already ventured into the water, including Sisuca. Essence sighed, nodding. "I'll miss you guys." The small group of girls nodded in turn, staring shamefully at the ground. "Bye, then." Essence waved, flashing an encouraging but sad smile before she turned and continued to progress deeper through the water. Alli knew the smile she had given them was fake because an escaped tear slowly ran down her face.

Ryker was having a hard time touching the bottom of the rock bed when they reached the center of the creek. The swirling water reached the middle of his torso, and Alli could tell it nearly swept him off his feet. She would have to keep an eye on him.

Alli had just searched their group to see if everyone was there before she heard a yell. Ryker had been swept under. Ruby screamed her brother's name, and Archie, who was a strong swimmer, dove below the frigid water, grabbing Ryker and pulling him to the surface for air. Archie swam toward the bank as fast as the strong current would let him, pulling the small boy along with him.

When everyone reached the opposite side of the creek, the pendant was once again unresponsive. But now, sitting on the bank, Alli wished it would warm her up again. Her body tensed again from the biting cold.

Suddenly, Ryker, who had curled up next to a pine tree, his clothes dripping wet, straightened. "Whoa," he said. "I feel . . ." He paused for a moment. ". . . warm all of a sudden." Alli suspiciously looked at the necklace, which showed no sign of doing anything at all. "Hmm," she grunted quietly to herself.

Kaimen curled up on the rocks and soon fell asleep. Many of their group followed his example since it was already around midnight. But Alli couldn't sleep. She was tired, yes, but she was too cold and too worried about finding the way home. They had already lost more than half of the kids they had started with, including Sisuca. They only had Essence, Ruby, Ryker, Riley, Kaimen, the blond boy Corrado, Miriam Hunt, Alli's mom, and Archie.

That was more than Alli thought when she counted everyone. But it didn't make the situation any less heartbreaking. She was surprised Sisuca had left since she was one of the most excited about getting home. Alli would miss the girl. She could still see that Essence was angry she had left.

While Alli looked up at the stars, she hoped they would find the orb and get home soon so she could rest again. She wanted to go back to her crazy, busy life that now seemed normal if she compared it to the eventful past weeks. Now her only obstacle was LeRouge's deal.

The wind blew and whipped Alli's pale, blonde hair around her face, the moon illuminating it and giving it a sort of silvery glow.

"*Alli.*" It was that sweet voice again.

"*I'm still waiting.*"

"*Come to me.*"

"*Alli.*"

"*Alli.*"

"*Alli.*"

Alli smiled. The voice, which she now found so comforting but also feared, faded once again.

Riley was curled up next to her, resting her curly head on Alli's lap, breathing softly. Alli ran a hand through the young girl's tangled curls before she leaned back against a tree and fell asleep.

CHAPTER THIRTY-ONE

The Cave

T he second day of travel was the longest day Alli had ever had. They'd already traveled an estimated 20 miles the first day. She hoped that today wouldn't be as far.

She began to notice that the farther north they traveled, the more often the necklace pulsed. But now it had stopped pulsing and hummed instead, staying warm against Alli's skin. They had left the woods and were trudging across a grassy field. The farther north they went, the more the charm started to burn like it had in Alli's dream. It was not quite as intense, but it burned all the same.

They reached the edge of a vast field. The grass reached past Alli's waist, almost completely covering the triplets. The plot of land had to be at least 20 acres. A rusty, stray tractor was parked in the center.

"Okay, everyone, we will camp here since we are nearing the end of the day and since we also don't know how much farther our journey will be. I need some of you to look for wood and others to start making food," Essence announced. Immediately, the triplets rushed into the woods in a flurry of red curls.

Alli smiled before she walked over to Essence. She put a hand on her friend's shoulder. "Essence, I'm going to go on a walk real quick. Is that okay?"

Essence turned to look Alli in the eye. "Sure. Are you okay?" she asked.

"Yup." Alli tried to sound cheerful. "Just have some things on my mind."

Essence didn't look convinced.

* * *

Alli started for the other side of the field, leaving her friends behind to set up camp. The setting sun shone down on her, warming her from head to toe as she trudged through the thick grass. As soon as she couldn't see her friends anymore, she bolted.

Alli sprinted as fast as she could to the other end of the field. She knew the cave was close. It had to be. The necklace pulsed and burned more intensely than it had before. It seemed to be urging her on like it was saying, "You're close. So close."

She plunged into the woods on the other end of the land. Alli didn't let the trees and brush slow her down. She leaped over rocks and logs and rabbit holes and small bushes until she came to a river.

The lush, grassy forest floor became a rock bank that bled into the calm river. The evening sun became blocked by a huge wall of rock that loomed over the water on the opposite side. Spruce and cedar trees grew like a crown on top of the majestic cliff.

Alli gasped when she saw a cave in the center of the wall. Immediately, she knew this was the cave. The orb was in there somewhere. They were going home.

Alli hurriedly untied her shoes, removed them, and peeled off her socks. She rolled up her jeans and started for the water when she noticed a small fern growing out of the rock bank. She froze and watched as it died. Her heartbeat pounded in her ears.

"So I'm assuming *that's* the cave," a sly voice said behind Alli. It wasn't a question. The girl turned to find Everit Graves standing behind her.

"You!" Alli snarled. "How did you find me?"

"Followed you," he replied as if that was the obvious answer.

Alli's face twisted into a scowl. "What are you here for?" she asked.

"To find the last orb. LeRouge is smarter than you think. She knew she couldn't trust you to actually *destroy* the orb, so she sent me to make sure you held up your end of the bargain." He smiled cruelly. "Technically, I wasn't supposed to show myself. But you know how it goes. *I* want to be the one to destroy the orb instead of letting some little girl have all the fame. So I have improved LeRouge's plan."

He pulled a red orb out of his cloak. "You see, I will tell LeRouge that you went back on the deal and tried to get back home, but since her trustworthy spy was there, he stopped you all and was forced to put you in jail. And then *I* will get the privilege of destroying the orb. LeRouge will be proud of me. Everyone from both Night and Order will accept me as their leader. So, you see, it's simple. No one will ever find you again, and you will be left alone in a dark cell." He smiled and raised the orb to the sky as he started speaking in the babbling language.

Alli backed away from Graves where he stood staring into the red orb, the scarlet light reflecting in his eyes. She turned and jumped into the freezing river, holding her breath as long as possible. The girl swam down . . . down . . . down.

The river became black and murky the farther she descended, and Alli couldn't see a thing unless it was right in front of her face.

The water pressed in on her, and the girl's ears popped. It felt as if knives were being stabbed into her brain. She couldn't stay under any longer. She had run out of breath, and her head felt like it was being smashed. Alli paddled for the surface.

She broke through and inhaled as much fresh air as her lungs would allow. Her blonde hair suctioned onto her face and neck. Her jeans unfortunately weighed her down. Alli had never been a strong swimmer in the first place. She gasped and glanced back at Graves who had stripped off his cloak and followed her in. He was only 10 feet behind her and was gaining fast.

Alli noticed that under one arm he still held the red orb, which glowed through the water. Everit Graves' gray-blond hair was plastered to his head, and a cruel, triumphant smile was etched across his face.

Why isn't he doing his flying thing? Alli thought. *Cannot everyone do it? Maybe it requires wearing the cloak too.*

The girl filled her lungs with air before she dove under again. She had to get to that wall. There was no way Graves could climb that without using two hands. He would have to either give up his precious glowing ball to follow Alli or let her go. It was Alli's only plan.

She swam with her eyes closed since it would be no use to open them under water. She couldn't see a thing anyway. Alli felt the ground start to ascend, and she broke through the surface once more. She stood and waded toward the wall.

Alli heard a splash behind her but didn't risk looking back.

"You will never escape me, girl!" Graves yelled from somewhere behind her.

Fortunately, Alli had reached the wall and started to pull herself out of the water, scaling it like an inexperienced spider monkey. The rock was slick, but the girl couldn't let that slow her down. She hoisted herself up, inch by inch, but her progress wasn't fast enough.

A strong hand wrapped around Alli's ankle.

"Ha!" Graves sneered. "I told you that you would never get away from me." He yanked her leg down. Alli cried out in anguish and fear. She gripped the side of the wall as if it was her only life support, which was partly true.

She panted, and her heart rate picked up speed. This was it. She was doomed. There was no escaping him. She would be sucked into the orb and put in a dark cell, never to see broad daylight again.

Alli's fingertips ached. She could feel her body slowly starting to tire. She wouldn't be able to hold on much longer. She had to do something.

Using only her arms to keep herself from falling, Alli kicked Graves in the nose with her free foot.

"Gah!" He let go of her leg and dropped the orb into the water, clutching his bleeding nose. The orb sank to the bottom of the river, the scarlet glow fading until it disappeared all together in the depths of the water 15 feet below the surface.

While Everit was distracted, Alli continued to climb. She realized the cave was directly above her, and reaching that cave became her new goal. She only had 10 more feet to go.

The wind whipped wildly around Alli's body. She tried to ignore it. She couldn't start worrying about the wind—not now.

Alli willed it not to sweep her off the wall and fall into the river 10 feet below.

Ten minutes later, she reached the mouth of the cavern.

* * *

Alli stood at the gaping mouth of the cave. This was it. This was the cave from her dream. She knew it because the necklace started to pulse and turn warm. She itched to go in and find the orb that would take her home.

But first she needed to get everyone else. She turned and stared back down at the water that flowed 25 feet or so below her. At this height, she could see the woods. Beyond that she could see part of the grassy field. It was an amazing view. She knew that if she had time, she could sit there all day watching the wildlife from afar.

Graves was gone. He had disappeared. Alli couldn't help but wonder what had happened to him.

Well, at least I'm safe, she thought. *Now I just have to climb back down to go get the others.*

She shivered. Down seemed more terrifying than up, but Alli would have to do it sooner or later. She couldn't leave her friends behind.

She started to climb down the wall.

* * *

"Guys!" Alli shouted from the middle of the field. "Come on! I found it!" She waved her hands to grab their attention.

Archie dropped boiling water on the fire, snuffing out the flames as he jumped to his feet and ran to meet her. His dark eyes were wide and filled with hope.

"I don't believe it!" he cried. "Show me!"

Everyone else stopped what they were doing and ran to join Alli and Archie.

Alli's mom walked toward her daughter as fast as she could. Mrs. Hunt jogged to catch up with her. "Mom!" Alli ran to her mother and enveloped her in a tight hug. She could tell that Mrs. Cormac wasn't healed completely, but her fever had left her.

"Oh, Alli!" Mrs. Cormac had silent tears of happiness trailing down her pale face. "Please, show me the way there."

Alli tore off back the way she had come, everyone following her at the same speed. Even her mom raced after her. She coughed every few strides, and her breathing became ragged. But she ran with them all the same.

They all slowed down when they came to the wall where the cave sat 25 feet above them.

Everyone cheered, hugging one another. The triplets danced in a happy circle on the rocks, and Mrs. Cormac was smiling, standing straight. She hadn't coughed since she reached the river. Even Kaimen and Corrado had a smile planted on their faces.

Alli sighed, ready to go home.

Everyone was ready.

Everyone knew that now was the time.

No one wanted to wait because of the deep longing that filled their chests.

Essence nodded at Alli, her arms wrapped around Miriam.

The group swam across the river and climbed the wall.

CHAPTER THIRTY-TWO

A New Beginning

Alli led the group through the dark cave. She remembered how to navigate the tunnels from the dream. She knew where to turn, when to turn, and which passage led to the giant cavern they needed to reach.

Alli veered right down a dark tunnel. The ceiling was low and narrow, forcing people to crawl in single file except for the triplets who only had to bow their heads. Alli scraped her knees on the sharp rocks, tearing her jeans. She didn't care because she was so close to getting home that she was determined that nothing would stop her.

The tunnel ended ahead, and Alli saw something gleam even though it was dark as night in the passage. It was the trapdoor, the one from her dream.

Alli delicately ran her hands over the polished stone. It was beautiful. The hinges were made of gold. Swirling designs covered the edges around the door. There were patterns that emitted their own glow, illuminating Alli's pale and excited face.

"What's going on?" Kaimen asked. "Why the holdup?"

"Be patient," Miriam responded calmly. "Alli's getting there."

The boy huffed. "Whatever." Alli could hear the agitation in Kaimen's voice.

Why is he being so impatient? Alli asked herself. *We just got here!*

The girl started to sweat. She didn't know how to open the door, and Kaimen was getting antsy. Everyone expected her to know how to find the orb.

Alli ran her hands over the trapdoor once more, hoping to find a clue she had missed.

Her cold hands ran over a small nook that was engraved in the center of the stone. Alli cocked her head curiously, now tracing the outline with her finger.

Hmm, she thought. *It's about the size and shape of . . .*

Her necklace started to pulse again, and an idea occurred to her. She unclasped the chain around her neck and laid the pendant in the engraved area.

Heat filled the tunnel, and the pendant, along with the trapdoor, started to glow brightly, illuminating every rough edge in the passage. Alli glanced behind her, checking to see if anyone else had noticed the bright glow. Archie, who had been following behind her, was lying on his stomach, resting his head on his arms. Essence had sat down, legs crisscrossed like Alli's mom and Miriam Hunt. Kaimen as well as Corrado were nowhere to be seen. The triplets were curled up together, smiling and waiting patiently for Alli to finish. "You can do it, Alli," Ruby encouraged her.

Alli nodded and turned back to the trapdoor that shone more brightly than it had a minute ago. She reached out to touch it, and without warning, the trapdoor disappeared into thin air. Alli tumbled through the opening.

She didn't have time to yell before she hit the rock below her. The girl landed on her shoulder awkwardly, and she heard a crack that faintly filled the cavern. Alli attempted to sit up but was forced to lie back down on the cool, jagged stone floor as a sharp pain coursed through her arm and neck.

Archie poked his head through the circular hole. "You all right?" he asked.

"Yeah," Alli responded, wincing when she forced herself to stand, despite the pain in her left shoulder. She sucked air in through her teeth, willing herself not to cry.

Archie was already dropping down through the hole, followed by Essence, Mrs. Cormac, Miriam Hunt, and the triplets. Archie helped lower the small siblings down.

They were the only ones who came through the hole.

Alli frowned. "Where's Kaimen and Corrado?"

Ryker stared at her. "They left. They said something about how they were tired of waiting for something to happen."

Essence looked defeated. She had wanted everyone from the Pentagon to make the journey with them until the end. But she couldn't control them or what they wanted to do. Alli clutched her shoulder with her right hand, trying to prevent it from moving while she walked to the end of the cavern where she could see light up ahead. She was excited. They were almost there, only 100 yards away. She could make it.

Alli didn't know where the necklace had gone. She hadn't been able to find it after she fell. All she found was a pile of ashes under the hole in the ceiling.

Essence briskly walked beside her. Alli could tell that her friend was itching to run ahead toward the light, but she stayed by her side, smiling with delight.

Archie trailed along behind them, staying with the two mothers. The triplets ran through the vast cavern playing a game of tag. An excited air filled the towering cave, and Alli couldn't hold back her delight any longer. She ran toward the light, which she now saw was an orb that floated three feet off the ground. The orb was white and gold and gave off a blinding light, unlike the darker-toned orbs of the Night and Order. Her heart swelled with fear as well as a longing she had never experienced before. The light was calling to her, beckoning her to approach it.

She was close enough now that she could feel heat radiating off the spherical object. Alli watched as small particles swirled around the orb, slowly making the glowing ball swell until it became as big as a doorway. It was the most beautiful sight she had ever seen. She glanced back, making sure her friends were following her.

Then Alli realized they weren't friends to her anymore. They were her family. She would wait for them even though she wanted to rush forward and go through the light. But she would wait. She had waited for what had felt like so long, so she could wait a few more seconds.

Everyone caught up to her, and Essence grabbed Alli's hand, squeezing it tightly. Alli smiled. Then she realized she could move her shoulder and arm freely without pain. The closer she got to the light, the more it healed her shoulder.

Miriam took Essence's free hand, and Alli's mom laid her hands lightly on Alli's shoulders. Ruby wrapped her arms around Alli's waist. Ryker held tightly to Riley who had slipped her small hand into Miriam's.

Everyone's faces beamed as they started for the doorway. But before any of them could walk any farther, a flash of multicolored light struck the ground, leaving a scorch mark on the rock floor. It took Alli a moment to realize that the flash was lightning, and the lightning was no ordinary lightning.

"*Alli,*" a voice called, and around 15 cloaked figures appeared. All of them held orbs. All of them were there for one reason. Unfortunately, Alli knew that reason.

"I see you went back on our deal." LeRouge stated. "Tsk, tsk, tsk. It was a good thing I never trusted you, but still, *so* disappointing." She shook her head. "But now it looks as if *I* will have to destroy it."

LeRouge turned her attention away from Alli and stared at the golden orb. "Ah, *there* it is." LeRouge said. "I have been waiting for a long time to destroy you." She acted as if the orb were alive. She stepped closer to the sphere and pulled out her own black orb. "Finally, I can use my orb for what it was meant to do." She muttered into the black ball and thrust it toward the golden orb. But before anything could happen, someone behind Alli yelled, "*No!*"

Graves charged through the kids from the Pentagon, pushing them aside. He raced toward LeRouge and tackled her, knocking the black ball out of her hands. LeRouge regained her footing and punched Everit Graves in the gut. "Everit!" Miriam yelled. Alli glanced at Miriam Hunt. She looked surprised to see him there.

"You fool!" LeRouge cried.

Everit clutched his stomach, gasping for breath. "*I* was supposed to destroy the orb. And they weren't supposed to be here. Night was going to take all the credit for destroying the orb, and then we would be praised for it. But no, the stupid Order always has to interfere. I'm tired of playing your games, Dementia. You were never meant to be a leader," he sneered. "I will destroy the orb, and no one can stop me!" He lunged for LeRouge's black orb that lay forgotten on the floor.

"You fool!" Dementia LeRouge screamed again as Graves stood back up and whispered into the black orb. He turned to face her, an evil smile on his face. The woman shrieked in rage as she disappeared from the cave.

Alli turned her attention back to Graves. His chest rose and fell as if he had just run a marathon. His eyes gleamed in triumph. "It's time," he told the cloaked figures. Graves turned his attention to Alli. "You will never get home. You will be imprisoned here."

He smiled cruelly.

Everit Graves approached the golden orb that hovered peacefully above the ground. He muttered into the black orb, and the golden object began to vibrate. Graves laughed as the glowing sphere started to flicker as if it were losing its color.

Essence and Alli came out of their shocked daze. Essence charged Everit Graves, which caught him by surprise. He yelped when Essence leapt onto his back. She stole the black orb from his hands and chucked it at a rocky wall. The orb shattered to pieces, landing on the floor in a pile of shards.

Alli ran toward the rest of the Order and Night followers who backed against the cavern wall. She charged at the nearest cloaked member. They yelped as Alli grabbed their blue orb and threw it on the ground where the glass exploded into a million pieces. Archie and the triplets realized what Alli was doing and followed in pursuit.

Some of the cloaked members disappeared when they realized what was happening. Others tried to fight back by whispering into their orbs. But it was too late. After a few minutes, all the orbs were shattered, and as each orb broke, its owner disappeared—all except one.

One last cloaked figure remained, and Alli knew who was hiding behind the dark folds of fabric. She also noticed that the figure was trying to escape through the tunnel above them. The figure was about to hoist himself up when Alli yelled, "Stop, Charles Hayes!"

The figure obeyed, turning to Alli. "Why should I listen to you, little girl?"

She ignored his "little girl" comment. "Because I believe you owe an apology to everyone left in this room," she said.

Charles chuckled and lowered his hood, revealing his face, which was twisted into a scowl.

"You think you're so smart," he sneered. "I don't owe anyone an apology because I know I did the right thing."

With that, Charles pulled himself through the hole in the ceiling and disappeared before Alli could say anything more.

"So sad," Archie said miserably. "He felt like a father to me."

* * *

Everyone turned and walked toward the orb that lay on the floor of the cavern. Alli reached down and picked it up. The light flickered like it was losing its power. She ran her hand over the smooth glass and gasped.

There was a crack in the orb. Tiny golden particles leaked out of it like golden blood, floating around in the air for a few seconds before they disappeared. "No," Alli whispered. They had come all this way. The orb couldn't be destroyed. It was their last hope.

Her friends gathered around her as the orb flickered one last time, casting shadows around the room. Then the light seemed to shrink in on itself before it was gone. Essence put a hand on Alli's shoulder, and Mrs. Cormac rested her chin on her daughter's head. The triplets all hugged each other. The redheaded girls started to cry. Poor Ryker even looked defeated. Miriam Hunt grasped Archie's arm in despair.

All was lost. There was nothing they could do. The group would be stuck in this dark place forever. The black orb must have done something to affect the golden one.

"Come on. Let's go back." Mrs. Cormac pulled Alli to her feet. "We'll figure something out." She tried to sound encouraging.

Alli nodded and followed the others toward the hole in the ceiling. She wiped a tear from her eye as she watched Archie hoist Riley up into the tunnel above. Alli realized she had failed. She thought she could get everyone home, but she had let them all down.

Alli glanced back one more time at the clear, colorless ball of glass before she turned to the hole in the ceiling. She was the last one to climb through.

"Here." Archie offered a hand down through the hole. "Let me help."

Alli extended her arm, grasping the boy's wrist. He was just about to pull her up when she hesitated. Did she just . . . hear something?

"*Alli.*" A voice called. "*I'm not gone.*"

Alli yanked her hand out of Archie's. The boy looked at her in surprise. "What?" he asked, astonished.

"A voice called to me," she said. She turned and stared at the colorless sphere.

"What on earth do you mean?" Archie questioned.

"I've been hearing it ever since I got the pendant," she said, her heart filling with hope.

Maybe not all is lost! she thought.

"Hearing what?" the boy asked urgently. He was staring at her as if she had gone mad.

"A voice. It's been calling me! I know what it is now!" Alli ran back to the clear, glass orb on the cave floor. She was just about to reach for the ball when golden light burst out of it. Alli shielded her eyes from the radiant glare until a few seconds later when it faded.

Alli looked back at the sphere, which once again hovered three feet off the ground.

"Archie, Essence, Mom, everyone," Alli shouted as she started to laugh and cry at the same time. "Come and look! We're going home!" She wiped a joyful tear from her eye.

Everyone jumped back through the hole to meet Alli. She stood, watching the glowing, golden orb. Her nerves jittered with excitement.

"*Alli.*" The voice spoke in her head. "*Do you wish for me to take you home?*"

Alli turned to her friends who flanked her on both sides. She looked each of them squarely in the eyes. She could see so much hurt and sadness and betrayal reflecting in their expressions, but she could also see hope. She didn't need to ask them if they wanted to go home. She knew by their expressions.

Alli nodded, and cheers rose up from the group.

"*So be it*," the voice said. The orb started to glow as it emitted golden particles. The light swirled around them, growing brighter and brighter until it filled the cavern. Instead of the light becoming a doorway, it reached out and wrapped around the group like a huge blanket.

Alli closed her eyes and smiled as she let the light carry her away, back home, leaving the evil and darkness behind her.

Epilogue

Kaimen and Corrado had been wandering through the cave for hours. They were lost, and Corrado was angry at Kaimen for convincing him to come with him. It was Kaimen's fault that Corrado had left in the first place. Yes, he had been frustrated that Alli wasn't opening that annoying trapdoor fast enough, but he shouldn't have left in the first place.

"Dude!" Corrado spun Kaimen around, grabbing him by his shoulder. "Are we almost out of this place yet?" Corrado complained, hatred boiling up inside him.

"Just gimme a minute! I know we're close!" Kaimen was angry at himself. Why in the world did he think it was a good idea to leave when they were so close to going home? Why did he think he could run? Why did he think he could do it himself? And now, because of him, they were lost in this cold, musty cave, wandering around in the dark with no way to get out.

The boys sat down on the cold floor of the tight tunnel. Corrado glared at Kaimen who had once been his best friend but was now someone he loathed.

Kaimen leaned his head against the rocky passage. Silent tears streamed down his face. He was lost. His best friend was mad at him. And he was angry at himself.

Why did he think he could do it himself?

He didn't know what to do now except sit there in the gloomy darkness.

That was exactly what he did.

* * *

The doorbell rang, and Jax barked madly as Alli leaped down the stairs to answer it. By the time she had gotten to the bottom of the steps and into the living room, her mom was swinging open their cobalt blue front door.

Miriam and Essence, along with Archie, were waiting on the Cormacs' front porch. Jax bounded over to them and put his gigantic paws on Essence's shoulders. The girl smiled.

It turned out that Alli's 70-some-year-old neighbors, the Shirleys, had seen Jax back at the Cormacs' front door two days after Mrs. Cormac was kidnapped. Molly Shirley knew it was Alli's dog and took Jax into their house until the Cormacs returned. As soon as Mrs. Shirley saw Alli come back, she gave Jax back to her. Alli had never been so happy to have her dog again.

Miriam Hunt carefully held a delicate crystal vase full of roses, a hopeful smile spreading across her face. "Good morning, Amira." Miriam shuffled her feet nervously.

Alli studied her mom's expression. Amira Cormac had completely recovered from their hard journey. What most baffled Alli was that she had healed as soon as she stepped into the gold light. She hadn't struggled since.

Amira beamed at Miriam, Essence, and Archie.

"Miriam," Alli's mom said, stepping forward and wrapping Essence's mother in a tight embrace. "I'm so glad to see you again," she said.

Happy tears trailed down Miriam's cheeks. "Me too. I'm so sorry."

Alli smiled at Essence and Archie. The three made their way to the back patio where the triplets were having yet another wrestling match. They seemed unable to find any other way to have fun.

When the siblings saw Archie and Essence, they abruptly stopped their game and ran to the two, wrapping them in a tight hug. Archie laughed and picked up Riley while Essence walked over to Alli after she had greeted the three. Essence enveloped her in a tight but brief hug.

"How are you doing?" she asked, pulling away.

"Great. You?" replied Alli.

Essence sighed dreamily. "I'm glad to have everything back to normal again. My mom is doing amazing. She has been so desperate to make it up to me that it's almost overwhelming. But I love her for that. Today she was so eager to bring your mom flowers and ask if they could become friends again that she woke me up so we could go to the store to buy them."

Alli smiled. "I'm happy everything is slowly mending. By the way, is Archie still staying with you and your parents?" she asked.

"Yes. Mom and Dad gave him our guest room in the basement to become his room. He likes it, I think. He's been telling everyone how weird it feels to be part of a family."

"Oh, good! We're keeping the triplets, I think. My mom loves them, and the siblings act like they've been in the family forever. All three of them have already started calling my mom 'Mom.'"

Essence smiled happily, staring at the triplets with a joyful twinkle in her eye. Then her smile faded. "So, not to be nosy or anything, but what did LeRouge mean when she said you went back on her deal?"

Archie walked over and joined the conversation. "I was wondering that too," he said.

Alli sighed. She knew someone would ask her about this one day. She rubbed a hand down the side of her face.

"LeRouge . . . she had been following us ever since we left the hideout. On the first day when I was walking behind everyone, she came out of the woods to meet me. She said she would make me a deal. If I would find the golden orb and destroy it, she would let us go free. But if I *didn't* destroy it, she would kill all of us. She warned me not to tell anyone." Alli hung her head. "I didn't know what to do. If I didn't agree, she would kill us. But if I did, we would be stuck there for the rest of our lives."

She looked up at Essence. "I'm sorry. I was so angry that you were meeting with your mom for secret meetings, but what did I do? I met with a member from the Order. I messed up. I'm sorry," she apologized again.

Essence's eyes looked sad when she nodded and told Alli, "Yes, you made a mistake. But we all did to some degree. Nobody is perfect. So the least we can do is forgive each other. So I forgive you."

Alli bowed her head. "I forgive you too."

"Well, I guess since you guys are my friends, I forgive both of you," Archie piped in, a wide smile planted on his face.

Essence laughed, which was a glorious sound to Alli's ears. Archie snorted, and the three of them hugged. It was a happy moment. Alli had two amazing people at her side. As she studied each of them, a smile on their faces and eyes shining, Alli couldn't imagine what she would do without such amazing friends.

The triplets paused what they were doing and joined the group embrace. Archie picked up Riley again, and the small girl hugged him. Ryker smiled, hugged Essence, and said, "I love my family." Ruby wrapped her arms around Alli's waist and grinned.

Mrs. Cormac brought out a tray of sandwiches and a pitcher of lemonade for everyone to share. Archie, Essence, and Alli sat down on the lawn chairs around the patio table, happily chatting while eating sandwiches and drinking fresh lemonade. The triplets resumed their wrestling match while Miriam and Amira talked the rest of the morning and all afternoon with the crystal vase of roses between them.

* * *

That night Alli walked up the stairs to her bedroom after the triplets had fallen asleep downstairs on the couch. They were going to have to figure out different sleeping arrangements for the siblings. They just hadn't gotten that far yet.

Alli's room was still a mess. Homework still lay on the floor, her bed was unmade, and the rock Ilene Tempest had thrown still sat on the carpet at the foot of her bed. The window was fixed. Someone must have repaired it for her. Someone had swept up the glass from her floor.

Alli changed into her soft, gray pajama pants and a plain shirt before she walked over to her window. The flowers on her window box were wilted and dead. Alli frowned and opened her window to pull them out. Looks like she would have to get new flowers.

She stared deep in thought at the moon. As terrifying and scary as her adventure had been, some things had turned out okay. She had made amazing friends, and now Essence's mother had turned good.

The girl happily sighed and walked back to her bed. Jax was curled up on the covers, waiting for her. She sat down on the mattress. She scanned her room one last time, a smile on her face.

"I'm so happy to be home, Jax," she told her dog.

Alli turned off her lamp and fell asleep.

www.ingramcontent.com/pod-product-compliance
Lightning Source LLC
Chambersburg PA
CBHW062112080426
42734CB00012B/2835